I0156368

NIGHT TRAIN LANE

The Life of NFL Hall of Famer
Richard "Night Train" Lane

MIKE BURNS

EAKIN PRESS ◆ Fort Worth, Texas
www.EakinPress.com

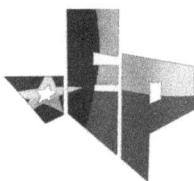

Copyright © 2000
By Mike Burns
Published By Eakin Press
An Imprint of Wild Horse Media Group
P.O. Box 331779
Fort Worth, Texas 76163
1-817-344-7036
www.EakinPress.com
ALL RIGHTS RESERVED
1 2 3 4 5 6 7 8 9
ISBN-10: 1-57168-440-9
ISBN-13: 978-1-57168-440-0

Library of Congress Cataloging-in-Publication Data

Burns, Mike
    Night Train Lane : the life of NFL hall of famer Richard "Night Train" Lane /
Mike Burns– 1st ed.
        p.   cm.
    Includes bibliographical references.
    ISBN 1-57168-440-9
    1. Lane, Richard, 1928- 2. Football players–United States–Biography. I. Title.

GV939.L29 B87 2000
796.332'092–dc21
[B]
                                                                                00-059303

CONTENTS

Highlights of Night Train's Career

PLAYING CAREER:
Los Angeles Rams (1952-1953)
Chicago Cardinals (1954-1959)
Detroit Lions (1960-1965)

PLAYED IN SIX PRO BOWLS

NAMED TO ALL-PRO 1ST OR 2ND TEAM 5 YEARS

5TH ALL TIME LIST—LONGEST PASS RECEPTION
98 yards completion from Ogden Compton (11/13/55)

2ND ALL TIME INTERCEPTION LIST
68 in career
Totaling 1,207 yards, and 5 TDs

MOST INTERCEPTIONS IN ONE SEASON
14 interceptions, L.A. Rams (1952)
Still holds the league record as of 1999

2ND ALL TIME LIST—
MOST YARDS GAINED OFF INTERCEPTIONS

3RD ALL TIME LIST—
PASSES INTERCEPTED IN CONSECUTIVE GAMES
6 passes intercepted
Chicago Cardinals (1954-1955)

ALL TIME NFL CORNERBACK—Named by
HALL OF FAME BOARD OF SELECTORS—1969—
first 50 years NFL History

INDUCTED INTO PRO FOOTBALL HALL OF FAME,
Canton, Ohio (1974)

INDUCTED INTO MICHIGAN AFRO SPORTS
HALL OF FAME (1986)

VOTED INTO MICHIGAN HALL OF FAME (1988)

COACHING EXPERIENCE:
Defensive Coach, Southern University,
Baton Rouge, Louisiana (1972-1973)
Defensive Coach, Central State University,
Wilberforce, Ohio (1973-1974)

FOREWORD

I first heard of Night Train Lane when I was a rookie in 1952 with the Chicago Cardinals. A small notation on a scouting report said, "Dick Lane, cornerback, 6'2", 185 lbs., Scottsbluff Junior College, Scottsbluff, Nebraska." The report didn't have any special notations. But, before that year was over, believe me, he was more than a notation. He would set a season record for intercepting passes, and would become well known as "Night Train."

I never knew why the Los Angeles Rams let him go, or what the Chicago Cardinals gave up to get him. But all you had to do was watch one practice, as I did, and you knew he was a special athlete.

He came to Chicago in 1954. "The Train" would cover receivers in practice like they were grammar school kids. Nobody ever beat him. Nobody ever caught a pass on him. When they would try to throw his direction he would either knock it down or intercept it. And then he'd laugh. No one ever knew why he laughed, but his constant laughing was taken as taunting or mockery by many, and they didn't like him because of it. I never figured it out, but it didn't offend me. It was such a contagious laugh, I thought he was just enjoying himself.

Some days he'd line up with the offense, and when the play started no one could cover him. He'd beat the best. At the end of practice we always ran sprints, then he'd beat everyone again. As I'd reach the finish line, there ahead of me was Night Train, laughing and looking back.

Memories of his abilities have never faded from my mind. Today they talk of "cover corner backs," people like Deion Sanders, whom no one can beat—the ones quarterbacks don't want to throw at. But, believe me, Night Train was better. He took chances on defense; smart, calculated chances. That's why the interceptions came so often.

And they talk about hitters, players like John Lynch at Tampa Bay, but they don't come close to "The Train." He covered receivers and tackled better than anyone ever has in football. When opposing runners broke free, they'd better know where #81 was on the field, because he was waiting to hit them. For someone no bigger than he was, he could deliver a blow as hard as I've ever seen. Many times I'd hear the sounds of his tackles throughout the stadium. They actually echoed across the field.

In defensive meetings he was very thorough in his preparations. Many meetings lasted longer because of "Train" questions. But because he asked so many of them, every one on the team was better prepared. He always put forth 100% in his game strategy and preparation.

He left the Chicago Cardinals the year after I did and we lost personal contact. Oh, I knew some of the things that happened to him, like his marriage to Dinah Washington and the continued reputation and respect other players had for him, but we didn't remain in close touch. I'd see him at National Football League Alumni Golf Tournaments and other NFL-related functions. I also knew he worked for the Detroit Police Athletic League (PAL), and his personal reputation in that arena was also outstanding. Each time we saw each other again, the first thing I noticed was his contagious laugh. It was always that laugh. Then later, we'd part ways.

Richard "Night Train" Lane. I played with him and against him. He was the best I've ever seen.

— PAT SUMMERALL
Chicago Cardinals (1952-1957)
NY Giants (1958-1961)
CBS Sports (Radio & TV) (1960-1994)
Fox Sports TV (1994-present)

ACKNOWLEDGMENTS

I need to thank three people who did extensive research and background investigative work which gave me excellent information surrounding dates, times, and places:

Coral E. Richards, Secretary to the Board of Governors, Western Nebraska Community College, Scottsbluff, Nebraska. Coral was able to come up with several names and phone numbers of people who attended Scottsbluff Junior College, Scottsbluff, Nebraska, in 1947. Her diligence enabled me to speak personally with these individuals who attended school and played football with Richard Lane.

Judy Stephenson, Technical Information Specialist, U.S. Army, Armor School Library, Fort Knox, Kentucky. Judy researched the voluminous data banks at the U.S. Library at Fort Knox, which provided insights into various army sports programs in 1948.

Pete Fierle, Information Services Manager, Pro Football Hall of Fame, Canton, Ohio. Pete utilized his extensive background knowledge at the Hall of Fame and thereby found many news articles dating back thirty years which covered the exploits both on and off the field relating to Richard Lane, and a listing of each football team and their yearly records.

A special thanks should be directed to Ed Eakin, owner of Eakin Press in Austin, Texas. Ed had the knowledge and foresight to see that this story was special enough to be told. He saw the inner struggle and the societal pressure that a person such as Richard Lane had to overcome to reach the pinnacle in his professional and private life.

CHAPTER ONE

COMMENTS FROM THE PROS

Probably the greatest accolade a professional athlete can receive is not linked to the number of games won or championships won. The greatest accolade has to be the recognition from one's peers in that particular sport. If this is indeed true, Richard "Night Train" Lane had to be at the head of the class.

Steve Sabol, president of NFL Films, said, "Night Train Lane was way ahead of his time in this league. He had a flair, a sense of bravado. He was the forerunner of Deion Sanders. In my all-time greatest defensive backfield, I have Willie Wood of the Green Bay Packers, Ronnie Lott of San Francisco, both playing safeties and Herb Adderly of Green Bay, plus Night Train Lane of Detroit playing the all important cornerback positions."

Sabol continued: "You've got to understand, Night Train perfected the clothesline tackle in pro football. He could go a whole season and not make a tackle below the jawbone. He and Ronnie Lott have got to be the two best hitters of all time."

Ronnie Lott, San Francisco's top defensive back, said, "I really thought I had a good chance at Train's interception record in 1986. I had eight interceptions through eight games, but I broke my leg and missed a few games that year. I only finished with ten interceptions for the year. We played a lot of passing teams back then and I really thought the record would be mine.

"But, to break that record, you've got to stay healthy and lucky. That's two hard things to accomplish in one season. One reason the record has stood for so long is, even with teams now playing 16 games in a season, it's hard to find a quarterback who will throw the ball consistently to the wideouts. You've got to remember, back in the early days of football, there were primarily only two receivers, so more balls went their way. That enabled the defensive backs to concentrate on those two players more."

Pat Summerall, longtime CBS and Fox sports broadcaster, played with Night Train in the days of the Chicago Cardinals and then against him for several more years. He noted, "Night Train had no idea how fast he really was. Ollie Matson was a very quick running back and Train was even quicker than he was. Every time we lined up on the Cardinals to run a footrace between our teammates, the Train always won. He just outran everybody, all the time."

Summerall continued, "They hardly ever used stopwatches back when I played, they just said 'everybody line up and run.' Once we all got situated on the goal line, ready to sprint to the other goal line, or maybe the 40 yard line, they'd just say 'Go!'"

Summerall remembered that in team defensive meetings Richard always asked the most questions and seemed the most eager to learn. "I know he had a reputation for being a gambler on defense, but you've got to understand, with his speed and defensive knowledge, he was an expert gambler in the best sense of the word. In tight game situations he usually made the right decisions at the right moment. If he happened to make a poor decision during a play, his speed usually made up for it.

"Night Train was a lot smarter than they gave him credit for, too," Summerall noted. "He was outwardly quiet and that led some people to think he was dumb. He knew more than he let on, and he was anything but dumb; he was quite intelligent."

As far as trouble on the field, Summerall recalled Richard always being on top of the situation. "Train never caused much trouble or fighting during the games, but when a fight broke out, he never backed down—never, not from anyone."

Injuries during the NFL season have always been the biggest concern of each team. Summerall remembered Richard as very seldom being hurt. "In the few instances when he was injured, he tried to treat himself in the trainers' offices. He had some distrust for the trainers, even though they were great people who did wonderful work. I never really understood that aspect of him. I'd see him with an ankle sprain as he limped into the office. The next thing I know, he's icing it down himself and then taping it. He'd just walk out, not saying anything to anyone."

Summerall recalled instances in the Pro Bowl, which at that time was played in Los Angeles, when Richard excelled against the best players. "All the fastest players practicing for the game liked to bet on who was indeed the quickest. After a practice, they would meet on the goal line, with each man putting up a small cash bet. Train lined up against all the receivers and defensive backs and they'd sprint to the other goal line. Not only did he regularly beat them, he did it with a great deal of flair. Lots of times, by the time the group reached the other 20 yard line, Train would be far enough ahead of them that he would turn around and run the remaining 20 yards backwards, waving at his pursuers as he did."

On recognition in the NFL, Summerall commented, "I've been around football since the modern era in the 1950s, and I'd rate him one of the top four defensive backs in history. He for sure deserved his recognition in the Hall of Fame."

Regarding Richard's induction into the Hall of Fame as a defensive back, Summerall said, "Train could have just as easily made it as an offensive receiver, but the coaches never utilized his talents in that way, which was probably a mistake. Year after year, everyone just marveled at his ability and game knowledge. I recall many times in practice we would be running offensive patterns and Night Train would step into the position of a receiver, just to keep his hand in that area of the game."

Summerall theorized Richard's preparation in his limited time on offense. "I think his practice time as a receiver enabled him to know their moves and thoughts more, which would enable him to cover them better in games. It was really funny, because on defense, he could cover anyone. And when he played offense, no one could cover him!"

Bob Mann, a Green Bay Packer receiver from 1950 to 1954, said, "Night Train Lane would just grab you by the head or face-mask and pull you down. I heard someone say something to him once, about that technique, and Train just said, 'I'd grab his eye-brows to get him down if I had to.'"

Alex Hawkins, a Baltimore Colts running back from 1959 to 1968, commented, "Night Train hurt you every time he made a tackle on you. He and Butkus were the toughest and hardest hitters I ever played against."

Red Hickey, a head coach at the San Francisco 49er's from 1959 to 1963, said, "Train was the greatest defensive back that ever played the game. Period."

Sid Gillman, the Rams head coach for 1955-1959, noted, "Richard Lane was the first back that could play the bump and run with receivers. He was just as fast as they were, if not faster. And his speed allowed him to gamble on plays."

Johnny Unitas, a Baltimore Colts great and Hall of Fame quarterback, once said about Richard, "Before one particular game, our coaches told me not to throw the ball to his side of the field. I told them I just couldn't give the guy a free ride like that. Well, sure enough, they were right, he picked off some balls that day and made us pay."

Detroit Lions tackle Alex Karras, 1958-1970, simply said, "Train was a great, great player. He for sure deserved to be in the Hall. And he was a really funny guy. He always broke me up with his antics and comments."

A commentator from ESPN once said, "Richard specialized in high tackles and vicious head hits. His motto was 'Hang 'em high!' His signature head shot was legendary in the league. The clothesline tackle was outlawed mostly due to him."

Tom Fears, a Los Angeles Rams receiver from 1948 to 1956, said, "Train was on my Rams team when he broke into the league. He immediately made an impact. It was easy to see his athletic ability. When he left the Cardinals and then onto Detroit, you had to think about him. He could hurt you."

Pat Studstill, Detroit Lions receiver, 1961-1967, explained,

"Night Train could just kill you!" He wouldn't tackle you fairly. He made the head tackle illegal in the NFL. He would just reach up and pull you down by the neck. That was known as the "Night Train neck tackle."

The accolades could go on and on. Night Train Lane was a legend among his peers. Quite an accomplishment for a man who began his life as a throwaway in a trash can.

Chapter Two

AN UNWANTED
CHILD

Austin, Texas, in the early 1900s was a small town. It was a place where families could raise their children with strong family values. Richard Lane, an African American, was born at Brackenridge Hospital on April 16, 1928. His mother, Johnnie Mae King, was a street walker, a prostitute. Johnnie Mae came to the hospital alone. The father of her new baby was a pimp, known simply as "Texas Slim." Slim didn't want the child and he certainly didn't want to pay any hospital bills for "one of his girls."

Johnnie Mae took care of Richard as best she could under the circumstances. Slim still had her working the streets of East Austin and expected her to bring in the money, baby or no baby. Slim was working the streets as a hustler, where he "rigged" card games and played street craps with anyone who had extra money. Slim told Johnnie Mae, "I'm working the streets too hard every day to be listening to a crying baby. Either the baby goes, or you go!"

Johnnie Mae knew deep down inside that the streets were no place to raise a child. She, along with Slim's other girls, traveled the "circuit" between Texas, Oklahoma, Missouri, and Nebraska. Slim would make sure they were in the right town at the proper time, when all the crops were being harvested by the farmers. This would enable them to get the farmers into pool hall games, street craps, or poker games. And it would allow his girls to "get close to every man they could."

It was a late summer afternoon in 1928 when Johnnie Mae reluctantly walked up to the large trash dumpster behind a row of houses in the 1900 block of East 9th Street. In her arms she carried three-month-old Richard, crying as usual. She glanced around to see if anyone was nearby, then quietly put Richard into the dumpster, covering him with some newspapers. She turned and walked away, crying as she went, constantly glancing over her shoulder at the dumpster, not really sure of her decision.

Ella Lane, a widowed black woman with two children, was sitting in her house at 1914 East 9th Street when she first heard the noise. She later told neighbors, "It sure sounded like a hurt cat to me. It was crying real loud." Ella walked out her back door, then down the alley, right to the dumpster. A second later, she saw it wasn't a cat at all. She couldn't believe it was a three-month-old baby. How could anyone do such a thing?

Ella talked to everyone she could, trying to find out who left the child. No one really knows why she didn't call the authorities to come get Richard; perhaps she just felt sorry for him. The real truth will probably never be known, but things were already looking up for little Richard. He couldn't have found a better home or a better mother than Ella Lane. Ella was religious, hard working, and honest. She worked long hours to take care of her children, Lincoln and Ora. With the addition of Richard, that one more mouth to feed was all right.

Richard was formally adopted by Ella Lane and became a member of her family. As he grew up in the neighborhood, people would tell Ella that the prostitute, Johnnie Mae, was asking questions about his welfare. Ella talked to everyone she could trust, and she came to believe that Richard was indeed Johnnie Mae's child. Ella didn't approach Johnnie Mae. She figured that anyone who would leave a child in a dumpster didn't deserve any input into the child's upbringing. Besides, Johnnie Mae never came directly to the house; she just talked to various neighbors. Ella knew that Johnnie Mae was working for Texas Slim, a violent pimp. It wouldn't be wise to get him involved.

As Richard grew up in Ella's house, he was introduced to proper church activities and good families throughout the neighborhood. When he was old enough, he immediately started contributing to the family's income by doing various chores for Ella like washing laundry, cleaning houses, boiling water, emptying wash tubs, making soap, cleaning out the chicken coops, and running errands for anyone who would pay him. Ella knew the fair value of a dollar and instilled this into her kids. Ella also did odd jobs for several white families in the area. Richard stayed by her side and assisted whenever he could. "Mama Ella was a hard worker, but very fair," Richard later said. "All the kids really loved her. We would do almost anything to make her happy. Her whole life she constantly sacrificed everything for us."

Ella's house wasn't big by any standards, but she always had an extra room for boarders or students who needed a cheap place to stay. Every few years she would save up enough money to have an additional room built onto her house. She would save all she could for materials, then promise to work for the local carpenters, cleaning and cooking, if they would provide the manual labor to build the new addition. It wasn't fancy, but it was another room for Mama Ella to rent out, weekly or monthly. All the extra boarders increased Richard's workload, but he didn't mind. "I knew that what I was doing would keep the family going," he later noted.

Life was normal for Richard and his adopted family in East Austin. He formed close friends that would be around him forever. Ella didn't have any extra money, but her family never suffered because of it. Richard said, "Mama Ella would always take care of us, no matter how bad it got." When he wasn't working to make ends meet around the house, he and his newfound friends played street baseball and any games that they could dream up. They never lacked for entertainment.

As Richard reached age nine, Johnnie Mae suddenly started appearing in the neighborhood. She was asking questions about him, Ella said. So, Ella just kept saying it was a lady friend of hers that cared about the family. Finally, a few times when Johnnie Mae came by, she left money for both Ella and little Richard. Richard started asking questions like, "Why did that lady give me some money?"

Ella would just say, "She's a friend of ours and she knows we need it."

As time went by, Johnnie Mae visited more frequently. On occasion she would spend some time with Richard, then go inside the house and talk to Ella for extended periods of time. She grew more friendly toward them both.

At about age eleven, Richard started asking more questions, and finally Ella gave him the news: "Richard, that lady is your real mother." Richard was shocked, not really understanding how his real mother could live somewhere else. Mama Ella simply explained that Johnnie Mae had left him near her home when he was a toddler, saying she couldn't take care of the baby. It was much later that Richard learned he had been abandoned in a trash bin.

Several times over the next few months Richard wanted to know who his dad was, but Ella only said, "It's a friend of your mom's. His name is Slim." Richard talked to several friends in town and they told him that Johnnie Mae worked for a man named Texas Slim.

When Johnnie Mae came by to see Richard, he started asking about Slim, but she wouldn't tell him who it was. Again, Richard went to his friends on the street and they eventually told him that Johnnie Mae was a prostitute who worked for Texas Slim. This was very hard news for Richard, but he had a good family with Ella Lane and he made the best of it. Richard later said, "I never made any attempt to meet my dad. I figured if he didn't want me around, I didn't want to see him either." Richard did not even know what Slim's name was.

Chapter Three

GROWING UP
IN AUSTIN

Richard's earliest recollection of a "real paying job" was somewhere around age eleven or twelve. "Somebody told me I could make lots of money working as a waiter and room service boy at the Stephen F. Austin Hotel," he later recalled. "I went down to the hotel and told them I'd do any work they wanted."

The Stephen F. Austin Hotel was a bustling enterprise around 1940, and private room parties were quite popular with anyone who could afford them. Richard worked for the head chef in the kitchen and did manual labor for the room service people. "I loved working at the Austin Hotel," Richard said. "When I worked for the chef I usually got to eat for free and that was always good news for a kid that grew up like I did. It wasn't real hard work, and I always knew a nice reward was waiting around the corner—some free food."

When a private room party took place at the hotel, Richard would get paid $1.25 to "service" the party. That meant he had to deliver all the food and drink trays upstairs to the rooms, then be responsible for cleaning up each room. Usually, after each party, some great food would be left on the trays. The chef always made it known that he wanted first shot at any of this expensive food, but if Richard had his way, that never happened.

One time, after a party upstairs, Richard was instructed to bring all the food trays out into the hallway and make sure to cover up any remaining food so that the chef could "check it out." Richard knew this meant the chef wanted it for himself. The chef was getting wise to Richard's tricks and quietly followed him upstairs. As Richard brought the trays into the hall he looked around for anyone in sight before he started eating off the plates. Suddenly, from around the corner, the chef appeared, "Ranting, raving and chasing me down the hall," Richard recalled. "I knew he couldn't outrun me so I just kept running until I heard him stop." A short time later Richard brought the trays into the kitchen and the chef had calmed down. "I was scared for a while, but everything was okay after I talked to him," he explained.

When jobs were scarce at the Stephen F. Austin, Richard went to work as a short order cook at the Nighthawk Restaurant. His training at the Stephen F. Austin was good, which enabled him to move up a notch and handle minimum cooking orders. At that time, the Nighthawk was one of the few premier restaurants in Austin, and having this job was a good break for a young kid. He had been taught how to make a nice dessert for himself by one of the chefs, and whenever the opportunity presented itself he would take advantage. Richard noted, "Back then it was real common to take a glass of iced tea, put some shaved ice in it, then add some vanilla ice cream or some half and half cream. We'd mix it up real good and drink it real slow, to make it last. We called it a tea milkshake. It was wonderful!"

Back in the 1940s and 1950s Austin was just like any other town with lots of kids. "We all formed street gangs and we all had our territories," he explained. "Of course, our territory was mostly east of downtown." The gangs back then weren't really violent gatherings. Most of the arguments were settled with kids' fists. "A few times, someone would pull a knife, but it usually never got too bad," he noted. "One time, some boys from another gang got mad at me and started chasing me. I ran and ran, finally jumped a fence and they lost sight of me, but I ran into a clothesline wire and it knocked me cold. I woke up bleeding and dazed," he continued, "but they never caught me. One of my buddies said, 'Well, looks like little Lane was too fast for them boys, but not fast enough for that clothesline.' From that point on, they called me Little Lane."

Most of the guys in Richard's gang hung out in pool halls and local parks around town. Richard liked to play pool and got pretty good at it. Good enough, in fact, to start making bets on pool games. The bet was usually ten-cents-a-game. During one game, Richard got the best of his opponent and started to collect, when all of a sudden the other kid started running toward the door. Richard picked up a cue ball, threw it, and "Beaned the kid right on the head. He hit the floor real fast," Lane said. "Then, all of a sudden I've got two nicknames—Little Lane and Cue Ball. I remember the kid's mother called the cops on me, but they didn't want to arrest a kid my age."

Toward the end of one summer, Richard was playing quite a bit of sandlot football. One day Ella surprised him with a nice new tweed suit to wear to church. She made it very clear he wasn't supposed to do anything to jeopardize that suit of clothes, especially playing football. Ella told him, "Richard, now I don't want nothing to happen to this suit for a long time, you hear me? And take care of those new shoes too."

"Yes, ma'am," he replied, knowing full well he wasn't going to put much effort into this promise. "Well, as luck would have it, one Sunday afternoon I'm walking home and there they are, some of my buddies, playing ball. Now what do I do? The next thing I know, the tweed jacket is hanging on a nearby fence post and it looked real safe there. I then took off my new shoes and felt pretty safe about playing. Heck, I had played barefoot plenty of times."

A short time later, after a few good tackles were made, one of his buddies yelled out, "Hey, Cue Ball, look at your pants!"

Richard looked down and saw nothing but grass stains all over him.

A few minutes later another pal said, "Hey, man, your pants are ripped too."

About that time, the entire group started laughing at him. But Richard didn't think it was too funny. He knew what was coming. "I walked over to the fence post to get my tweed jacket.

At least it still looked good. I picked up my shoes and slowly walked home, fearing the worst."

Upon his arrival at home, he tried to slide past Ella, but it wasn't to be. She was just too sharp for him. "Richard! Why you holding that jacket that way?" she asked.

"What way, Mama?"

"You got it wrapped around your waist like that."

"It's nothin'," he replied, walking ever faster. A few seconds later he was cornered in his bedroom, the evidence abundant. Ella started yelling and screaming at him, "Richard! What did I tell you? Huh?"

Richard just hung his head in silence, knowing nothing he said would work.

"Richard, I swear, I'm gonna kill you!" she yelled.

Ella left the room and came back with a leather belt. "Just perfect for whipping me," Richard said. "I'm yelling and screaming so loud, some of the neighbors yelled over the back fence at her 'Ella, what you doin' to that boy?'" He continued, "I'm just sure they thought I was being murdered. And to tell you the truth, it felt like it too!"

Years later, Richard would reflect back on that day and the beating he took. "It was a heck of a beating, but you know what? I scored so much in that game, I think it was worth it. And, after that day, I think Mama Ella saw how much I loved to play football, because she never really argued with me too much about it anymore," he noted.

Richard recalled his first organized sport being softball. The boys played and the girls watched. He attended Blackshear Elementary School in Austin, and they played ball all the time. "I really liked playing in the outfield because I could run real fast and catch anything they hit," he said. "Sometimes I played first base and that was fun too." Richard was also a good batter, as he explained, "I could really hit some home runs. Every time we got behind in a game and I came to bat, the other team knew they were in trouble. And it was a good way to meet girls."

Sometime around the tenth grade, Richard realized he was running faster than most of the people he played with in any sport. It seemed like he was running and hustling in every activity he put his mind to. If he was playing in some game and needed more speed, he just ran faster; it was as simple as that.

In high school Richard started playing more sports, like basketball, track, and most importantly, football. On the high school basketball team he played the center position, while only standing at a height of six feet. "Back then, not too many people were real tall, even the ones who played hoops," he noted. Richard played with several other kids who were also excellent basketball players. "There were a couple of kids on our team that no one could keep up with," he said. "We would run the floor, pass off to each other, knowing that the other team couldn't cover our speed. I could easily jump up and hang on the rim. I loved to run the floor and pass the ball to whoever was open. I also had a great jump shot. It looked real easy, and lots of times it was."

Years later Richard would look back on all his athletic accomplishments at Anderson High School, always ranking basketball his favorite sport. "I guess I should have stuck with it, but things just didn't work out that way," he said. "We had some great coaches back then who knew how to play the game, and our players took advantage of everything." He continued, "Some of the guys were taller than me, but nobody could outjump me. Playing basketball really fit my personality too. It was fast-paced and allowed me to show what I could do with my athletic skills."

Basketball players usually ran on the track team too. The coaches kept in real close communication with each other, and some of the coaches even coached both sports. They watched Richard run in basketball and quickly told him he needed to go out for the track team. Well, it didn't take too much asking to get Richard to take up a sport that required him to run fast. Richard said, "I ran both the 100 yard and 50 yard dash at Anderson. I was very fast at both and really enjoyed track. It was as simple as lining up with your competitors and seeing who could reach the finish line first.

"Back then, nobody ever lifted any weights either. I wondered how fast I could have run if I had lifted. But that was the farthest thing from our minds. We always were told that weight lifting made you tighter and unable to run.

"Well, football came somewhat easy to me, since I played the other sports so well, but trying to get on the team was a big problem," he said. "I for sure wanted to play football with the high school team, because I had been playing sandlot ball and I knew what I could do. But the coaches saw how little I was and they were afraid to let me play," Richard explained. "Plus, Mama Ella thought I was too little and she didn't want to hear anything about me playing that sport. I had two big hurdles to clear."

Ella Lane could be heard throughout the house yelling at Richard, "I better not hear you been out playing no football!"

"But I'm real fast and they can't catch me," he yelled back.

"I don't care what you say. No kid of mine needs to get hurt playing football, and I don't need no doctor bills either."

Richard knew that Mama Ella couldn't watch him all the time, so he had to take his chances and just hope he didn't get hurt. Maybe then she wouldn't find out he was playing. Deep down inside, he knew the odds were against him pulling this feat off. Besides, how could he keep it quiet? He knew that given the chance, he could make the varsity team, no matter what the coaches said about him being too small.

So when Anderson football practice was set to start, Richard simply told them he had permission to play. The coaches gave him a stern look, but the word had gotten around that he was blazing fast in sandlot ball and no one could catch him. The chance was his, to either make the team or fail miserably. In his mind, failure was not a possibility.

The head coach at Anderson High School was W. E. Pigford. Two of his assistant coaches were Mr. Timmons and Mr. McDonald. They were stern coaches but fair men in every respect. All the players on the team liked and respected them.

"Coach Pigford had a nickname for everyone and mine was Cue Ball, you know, because of the pool hall deal," Richard explained.

The first day of practice was easier than Richard thought it would be. He initially told Coach Pigford he wanted to play offensive receiver only, but within a short time he made it known he wanted to "go both ways," which meant he wanted to play offense and defense. Playing on both sides of the ball was very common in that era, even up through the college and professional ranks.

Richard recalled lining up at the receiver position in practice and catching a few balls from the quarterback. "I made some cuts downfield a few times and looked over my shoulder. Nobody was near me. I looked at the coaches on the sideline. They looked amazed that even some of the senior players couldn't cover me. I knew then I could play ball with the team."

He continued, "A few times I ran some deep routes across the field. I told the quarterback just 'throw it out there and I'll run under it.' Sure enough he did and I made quite a few nice catches. I was so shifty on my feet I could just fake them out with my moves. It was sure fun to watch their faces. Here I was, one of the smallest guys on the field and it didn't matter.

"But sure enough Mama Ella's prophecy came true," Richard sorrowfully explained. "We were playing a game that first year and some guy clipped me. I never saw him coming. I missed a lot of games that year. It was sure bad to hear her say 'I told you so.' But I had come this far and I wasn't going back," he noted. "I think Mama Ella knew she couldn't stop me from trying. She didn't put up much of a fight after that."

The next year at Anderson was much different—and better. Richard excelled at basketball and track. And when football season came around, he couldn't wait to prove himself again. He told Coach Pigford he wanted to play defense as well, and when the first week of practices rolled around he proved he could do it. Pigford told him, "I want you to cover a couple of these fast guys we've got here on offense."

"Sure, Coach," Richard answered.

The first few passes were completed to one of their best receivers, but Richard handled the assignment easily. He covered them "like a blanket." When one of the receivers caught a long pass downfield, Richard quickly made up the distance and executed a good tackle. The coaches and all of his teammates were impressed.

"By the second year I was even faster than before," he said matter of factly. "It was like I could run in another gear if I needed to. Sometimes I would lay back and act like I wasn't covering the play too close just to get our quarterback to throw at the man I was covering. Well, it usually worked. He'd throw it and I'd either knock it down, or if I was lucky, pick it off."

Sometimes the coach would yell at Richard, sensing that he wasn't playing to his full ability on defense. But that couldn't have been further from the truth. "I was just trying to bait them, that's all," Richard said.

Lonnie Jackson, a teammate of his at the time, was a year older than Richard. Lonnie easily recalled his famous football partner. "I was a year ahead of him in school and I knew more about the game, but it was easy to see that Dick Lane possessed some great skills that most players didn't have," said Jackson. "You have to know the setting at the time. Anderson High School played in the statewide Prairie View Interscholastic League, which was made up totally of black schools across the state. Anything less than a state championship was a failure to us. In 1942 Anderson won the state title with an undefeated season. In 1944, Richard's second year on the team, the Yellowjackets went undefeated again, but were later disqualified for using an ineligible player who had transferred in from another school. It was a big setback for us."

Lonnie continued, "And in 1944 we had set the statewide defensive mark for fewest points allowed in a season. I believe it was 20 points. So, in 1945 the team was set to repeat its season again. Anderson had a great season and went into the state finals game against a tough team from Booker T. Washington High School in Wichita Falls. But our team wasn't up to the challenge." Anderson lost the game by a score of 12-2. Lonnie noted, "Back then, the school administrators usually flipped a coin to determine where the championship game would be played. In 1945 they played it in Austin.

"Overall, Anderson was a great school with some outstanding athletes for many years to come. Dick Lane was one of those people," recalled Jackson.

Richard remembered being late to football practice a few times and the price he had to pay for this mistake. "We lived about 20 blocks from the school and every afternoon I had chores to do before practice. Usually, I'd have to sprint the 20 blocks just hoping I wouldn't be late, but sometimes I didn't make it," he noted. "So, Coach Pigford made me run laps around the field even before practice started. I told him I had chores to do, but it just didn't work. Pigford still made me run the laps. He usually just said 'Hit the track!' If I was going to quit, that would have been the perfect excuse."

Good friends were just as important then as they are today, and Richard Lane had two of the best in Plato Creighton and Charles "Tab" Fowler. They did everything together: hunting, fishing, camping, picnics, and sports. "Plato and Tab were just like brothers to me," Richard said. "Their fathers looked out for me just like I was one of their own family. We spent as much time together as possible. Their parents really liked Mama Ella and we were all supportive of each other's families."

The three boys would wander down to the river bank with poles in hand. Sometimes they were able to catch enough fish to cook a good dinner. "Catching catfish or bass in the Colorado River was easy back then," Richard explained. "It seemed like every time we went down there we came back with fish. But, really, we had our bad days too. Our hunting was a little harder though. None of us could afford a .22 rifle, so we used our sling-shots to kill squirrels and stuff. Every once in awhile, one of the older kids we knew brought along his dad's rifle, but that didn't happen too much," said Richard.

"Of course, Plato and Tab were part of our street gang and we all fought for each other as well," Richard continued. "I recall a few times when we would go to a dance and one of us would get up the nerve to ask out a particular girl. Little did we know that the girl was taken by some other guy from another gang. A fight usually took place outside the building, but we all covered for each other. Nobody could do anything without the other two protecting him."

Although getting good grades in high school was important in the 1940s, a lot of the athletes didn't put in the proper amount of effort. Richard said, "It's kind of like today. Lots of the good athletes spend too much time on sports and not enough studying. You think you can do it all, but all you do is cheat yourself out of a better education. In some ways, being an outstanding athlete wasn't the best thing to be."

Chapter Four

GOING TO SCOTTSBLUFF, NEBRASKA

During his early years in Austin, Richard maintained sporadic contact with his biological mother, Johnnie Mae King. She made sure that he and Ella had some extra money whenever she could afford to give it to them. She had to be sure that Texas Slim didn't catch her giving any money to them under any circumstances. Slim had a violent history with his "girls," and he regularly beat Johnnie Mae.

For some time, Johnnie Mae had not kept in touch with Richard. About the time of his senior year at Anderson, Richard learned that a few years before, Texas Slim had beat Johnnie Mae after a confrontation. Later that night, Johnnie Mae had shot and killed him while he slept. A criminal trial had ensued, and Johnnie Mae was convicted of manslaughter and sentenced to several years in prison. This happened in another state, which was one of the reasons Richard never heard about it. Richard found out about her incarceration, but he decided not to go see her for various personal reasons.

A few years later, about the time Richard was graduating from Anderson, Johnnie Mae was released from prison. She contacted Richard and invited him to come see her, this time under much better circumstances.

Johnnie Mae had moved to Scottsbluff, Nebraska, and opened a tavern, along with her new fiancé, Ronald Moore. Richard talked to Mama Ella and she agreed that he should go see his real mother, even if it was in Nebraska, "which is a long way from Texas," she said. Richard had just graduated from high school and was not sure of his future. Although he wanted to go to college, a visit to Scottsbluff seemed just right at the time.

Upon his arrival at Scottsbluff, Richard was struck by his mother's newfound life and her new companion, Ronald Moore, who seemed to be a good man. The tavern in Scottsbluff was a seemingly nice place that attracted fairly good clientele, and Johnnie Mae was making extra money serving food to local families.

Johnnie Mae was happy with her new life and the fact that, for the first time, she had her son under her wing. Also, Richard liked the town setting and its people, even though it was primarily a white population. Johnnie Mae suggested, "Why don't you move up here with us and go to school at Scottsbluff Junior College?"

"How will I pay for the college tuition?" Richard asked.

"I'll pay for it myself. Ronald will help out too."

For the next few days Richard checked out the area closely. He made some inquiries into the Scottsbluff campus and the courses he could possibly take. Finally, he decided to make the move, so he returned to Austin to talk to Ella.

Ella knew something was different about him. He was making more decisions on his own, but it was clear that something bothered him. Finally, Richard broke the news to her, "Mama Ella, Johnnie Mae wants me to go live with her in Nebraska."

Ella was stunned, but not really surprised. "What will you do about your schooling?" she asked.

"She said she'd pay for me to go to a junior college up there. It looks like a good place to go to school," he answered.

For a seemingly long time Ella didn't comment. Then she responded, knowing full well that this decision could drive them apart forever, but that this was the proper decision to make. "Honey, if you want to go live with your mom, go right ahead then. You should get to know her better. But," she continued, "just remember all the right things I taught you. All the times I took you to church. You know by now which decisions are the right ones."

Richard hugged Ella, knowing he was leaving the place where he had grown up. He would also be leaving his close friends—maybe forever. The next week or so he made it a point to see each of them. He had every intention of returning to Austin, but he really didn't know how long it would be.

Upon his return to Scottsbluff, Nebraska, Richard came to the realization that he was one of only a handful of blacks in town. If he made the football team he would be the only black on the roster. Scottsbluff was a large farming community and like any midwestern town, football was at the core of its activities. He knew he had to play his best to make it.

At Johnnie Mae's house, she and Ronald Moore had made up their minds to pay for Richard's tuition. She took Richard to register for his classes at Scottsbluff Junior College and arranged for him to meet with the Scottsbluff Cougars head coach, Bill Putman. Johnnie Mae told Richard, "I haven't been there for you in the past, but I'm gonna make up for it now."

"Mom, I know things haven't been right between us before and I'm gonna try real hard to do my best here," he answered.

"You just go to school, make good grades and things will work out. Ronald is a good man and he's behind you all the way."

The day came when Richard went to see Coach Bill Putman. He walked into Putman's office and explained that he was a new student and wanted a chance at making the team. Putman told him if he could make the team it would be as a "walk-on," someone who gets on the squad without benefit of a scholarship. Putman told him, "Son, everybody plays both ways here and it's a small team, so you've got to be good to make it."

"Coach," Richard said, "down in Texas we always played both ways. Just give me a chance to play."

"Come back two weeks before practice starts when we hand out the uniforms, and I promise you, you'll get your fair shot. Just remember, we've got some good kids here and the competition is tougher than you'd expect. Just how much do you weigh?"

"About 165 pounds," he replied.

Putman just looked at him and made a face, as though his weight was a problem.

"Don't worry, Coach, I'll be here," sensing that he needed to make a point.

Richard knew what tough competition was in Texas. At Anderson High School, he had been one of many solid players on a totally black squad, several of whom were just as fast as he was on the field. He knew deep down inside he could make it, given the opportunity. Again, failure wasn't a consideration at this point for him.

The first few days of school went well for Richard. It even seemed as if the student population, which was 99.9% white, didn't even notice him. In reality, as Richard would learn later on, the people in Nebraska were so nice and friendly, the color of his skin made no difference to them—he was just another student. Richard quickly found out that there was one other black student at Scottsbluff, a girl. They became good friends over the school year, but only dated occasionally. He noted, "I was so worried about school and making the team the first few weeks that getting a date wasn't on my mind."

During his time at Scottsbluff, Richard continued to play baseball. He enjoyed the sport and its athletic requirements, especially the fact that he could play several positions equally well. He took the time to try to develop his baseball skills by working on his fielding and pitching abilities.

At the junior college there was an older student nicknamed "Popeye." Popeye and Richard would get together a few times a week and play catch, hit balls to each other, and work on any of their skills that they deemed weak. Richard loved to pitch to Popeye, and they would pick an unused baseball diamond near the school to work out. Richard recalled, "I loved to pitch to him. I could really fire the ball with some steam on it and I enjoyed hearing him holler when he caught it."

"Dammit Lane, you've got to get me some padding for this glove!" Popeye said.

"Hell, I thought you were tougher than that, boy," Richard replied.

"You need to stand down here and catch a few of these!"

"How can we do that? Me pitch and catch? How does that work?"

Richard recalled laughing at Popeye during these conversations. Popeye was a good ball player, but it was apparent Richard had too much arm for him. It finally got to the point where every time Richard told Popeye he wanted to work out, Popeye would start in on his excuse about needing that extra padding for his glove.

One day Richard was involved in a pickup baseball game with some of the students at the school. "We were really playing ball hard the past few weeks and I was playing at about the top of my game," he recalled. Little did he know that during the game, a baseball scout for the Kansas City Monarchs, a major league team in the Negro National Baseball League, had watched them play and had been very impressed by Richard's abilities.

Apparently, the scout had been in town and had inquired about any good prospects at Scottsbluff Junior College. Richard's name was at the top of the list and the scout had taken the opportunity to see the game, which was much to his liking.

Of course, even then some college rules existed that frowned upon students playing collegiate sports and also playing for a professional team. "You weren't supposed to take any money at all to play sports," Richard said.

The pro scout talked to Richard. "I really like what I see, son. Have you ever played any organized ball before?"

"No, sir," Richard answered.

"Well, I handle a lot of the scouting duties for the Kansas City Monarchs and their farm clubs. Are you interested in playing for us?" he asked.

"Yes, sir."

"You going to school here at Scottsbluff?"

"Yes, sir. I'm just starting school this semester."

"Just how old are you?"

"I just turned nineteen in April," Richard remarked.

"Well, I need to see your mom. Who is she?"

"Johnnie Mae Moore. She and Ronald Moore run a tavern in town."

"I think I already know her. I'll go by and talk to her for you."

They shook hands and parted ways, leaving Richard wondering if anything would ever develop from the conversation. A few of the players on Richard's baseball team asked him about the conversation, but he downplayed it. Richard knew that if the opportunity panned out, he wouldn't want the word to get around that he took money for playing organized baseball.

Later on, Johnnie Mae explained to Richard that the scout came by their house and said he wanted Richard to play baseball with the farm team of the Monarchs, the Omaha Rockets. The scout was going to pay Richard $2 a day for food and related expenses. Richard found out later, "The guy also struck a deal to pay Johnnie Mae some money if I agreed to play with them. I don't think she ever told me how much it was and if she did, I really don't remember. I didn't care. I was just real happy to be playing ball on any professional level."

A few days later the scout returned with Richard's new Omaha Rockets uniform. Richard recalled that it "looked real good. I was real proud to be wearing it. I knew lots of guys that were great ball players that never got the chance to play with any pro baseball team. I knew this was a good chance for me. Here I was in town only a short time and to get a chance like this was great."

Richard recalled discussing the name he would use then, so his true name wouldn't be listed by the team. "It really wasn't too much of a variation—it was Richard King. You know, Johnnie Mae's maiden name was King." He added, "We thought that would be okay, since most of the games would be played out of Omaha, Nebraska, or some other towns around there."

The first day with the Rockets, Richard met the entire team and its manager, a man named DeeDee. Richard remembered, "Back then the managers were just like our mothers away from home. They were responsible for the whole team, like what we ate, where we went, and our total schedule. Whatever DeeDee said we had to do," remembered Richard. "You just didn't argue too much with the team manager, especially if you ever wanted to move up to the big leagues later on."

During that first workout in Omaha, Richard was showing the players what he could do as DeeDee kept a watchful eye on it all. Richard threw some pitches to the catcher, who was impressed with his arm. "I put some good heat on them to show them what I had," Richard said. "DeeDee walks over to watch us and says something like 'Hell, that kids got a good whip on him!'"

Within a very short time, Richard made a lifelong friend on the team when he met outfielder Kenny Morris. "Me and Kenny hit if off real quick. We had similar backgrounds and we became fast friends."

The weeks went by and the Omaha Rockets kept a pretty grueling schedule of games. "Once we played 23 games in 16 days," Richard recalled. "It was a lot of fun, though, and the time went real fast." The team played games across Nebraska, Wyoming, Colorado, and Idaho. "It seemed like we lived in that bus," he said.

All of the semi-pro teams they played consisted almost entirely of black players. Every once in a while they would run across some good Mexican players and some solid Puerto Rican players. "Some of those boys from Mexico and Puerto Rico could really play some serious ball," he recalled. "They weren't very big guys, but they were really fast and they had some great abilities to field the ball."

He continued. "The Kansas City Monarchs were a black ball club in a league of black owners made up totally of black players. But the Monarchs were considered the premier team in the league. They had won about ten pennants in the All Negro League and their players traveled in a custom bus. They stayed at the best black hotels when they traveled. Satchel Paige was their best player back then and they always had huge crowds watch them play. For me to be playing on one of their farm teams was a big step in the right direction."

For a while, Richard didn't realize that there was a lot of gambling going on before and during their games. After a while he came to see these same faces that appeared at all the ballparks. He started to ask questions and was told by one of the other Omaha players, "Those guys are betting a big load on us today. We better win big for them."

"How much are they betting?" Richard asked.

"Several hundred bucks, at least," he replied.

"Can we bet some money too?"

"I wouldn't do it. DeeDee would find out," he said.

As the season progressed Richard noticed that when they went to the same cities to play repeat games, the same sheriff's deputies always showed up to watch them. He later found out that the deputies were working with the gamblers, "Giving them some protection." Also, the deputies were starting to bet large amounts on the games themselves.

Richard recalled playing one game in a small dusty town in Idaho. One of the local police officers walked up to his team as they exited the bus and said, "You boys better win for us today, because we bet the farm on you."

Richard noted, "None of our players said a word to him, we just kept walking toward the building."

The game was a tough one, with the local crowd yelling and cheering against the Rockets at every opportunity. At one point in the game, Richard was playing first base when a white fan from the other team walked out onto the field and stood right next to Richard. "The guy stood there for a full five minutes without saying a word. Then, all of a sudden he starts yelling and cussing at me, saying things like 'What's a nigger doing on this team anyway?' I'm wondering, is this guy nuts? We're all black!"

The verbal harassment continued for several more minutes, and all the while Richard never even turned to look at the man. Richard said, "Now if that guy had come up into my face I would have protected myself, but he was just a blowhard. I really don't recall any other instance in my professional career that equaled that moment."

Finally, a police officer walked onto the field and dragged the guy away. As he was being led away he continued his verbal tirade at Richard. "I'm sure the cops didn't arrest the guy since we were in his hometown and all, but it was real nice to see them drag him off. Everybody in the stands was yelling and laughing."

The Rockets won the game, much to the satisfaction of Richard and his teammates. Afterwards, Richard saw one of the cops walk up to DeeDee and whisper something, then DeeDee gathered the team around him in the locker room. "Boys, we gotta get outta town fast. Appears some money was lost on account of us today and the guys coughing up the cash aren't happy."

"Hell, it's our job to win, ain't it?" one Rocket player said.

"Yeah," DeeDee responded. "But I guess not too many teams score 18 runs in one inning on that bunch."

"I'm glad we did too!" another player yelled.

"Yep, and I'm proud of the way you did it too," he answered.

The argument was short-lived and DeeDee immediately ushered them onto the Rocket's bus and told the driver to take off. "We didn't even have time to take a shower," Richard said. "I was kind of scared, to tell you the truth. I looked out of one of the bus windows and saw a small group of men looking at us and I didn't say a thing."

As they pulled away, DeeDee told them, "Pull all the window shades down, just to make sure." The bus sped out of town and didn't stop until they reached the safety of the next small city. Richard recalled them stopping at "some burger place and buying all the hamburgers they had on the grill."

On another road trip, after playing a double header, they stopped to get something to eat. "We all piled off the team bus and went up to the window of this fried chicken place out near some park," Richard said. "We had just sat down at these wooden tables when these two white women next to us started fighting over something. They started yelling and screaming and the next thing I know they're knocking over tables and chairs. Fried chicken was flying everywhere and we all grabbed our food and just backed up. They didn't even notice us. It was real funny. I sure wasn't going to lose my only food of the day to those two crazy women!"

Richard recalled, "Somebody figured out we drew more attendance to the games by having us play them in towns that had a county fair in progress or even the rodeo. Some of those people that went to the rodeos were really wild. I guess they were used to yelling at bulls and horses so they just yelled at us the same way." He laughed. "Lots of times when we played games at the fairs, we stayed around later on and spent all our money. But we had a real good time.

"Back in Omaha, when we played home games, the local deputies took real good care of us, especially when we won. Several times after games they would come by to give DeeDee some money they had won betting on us," Richard recalled. "They would say, 'You boys deserve a little of this, you made us some cash and we'll take care of you.' Then DeeDee would give us between two and five dollars."

Traveling with the Rockets was an experience in itself. Lots of towns they visited wouldn't accept black, Mexican, or Puerto Rican players in their hotels, so usually the entire team would just sleep on the bus. Taking a shower was also a constant problem. If the showers didn't work in the ballparks, they just got on their bus and drove around until they found acceptable facilities. Sometimes they never found them, so they just stayed dirty and sweaty until the next day.

Many times on those road trips, the white gamblers following the team would suggest a "whites only" café. All minority players would be excluded from the café, so the gamblers would go inside and order food for the entire team. "Once in the bus they just gave the food to us," he noted. "It was just a part of life to me. A part I didn't agree with or like, but a part I couldn't control."

One time Richard and several Rockets players were walking a few blocks from the ballpark where they were going to play later that afternoon. It was a "whites only" place to eat, but Richard said, "Me and my friends were real hungry, so I just walked inside. My buddies stood in the doorway and didn't enter. They didn't say a word. I sat down at the counter as everyone in the place just stared at me. A second later, the white cook walks out with a meat cleaver in his hand and he starts threatening me with it," Richard remarked. "I got real mad and picked up a chair to hit him with, you know, just for protection. As I backed toward the door I heard my buddies telling me to drop the chair and run. Once I reached the doorway I threw it at him, then turned and ran out the door. I wished that cook didn't have that cleaver in his hand, so I could have fought him fair." He paused to remember. "I kind of expected to see that guy at our game later, but he didn't show his face."

While on the road, Richard called Johnnie Mae in Scottsbluff, just to see how things were going. A letter from Ella Lane had arrived and she wanted Richard to come to Austin to see her as soon as possible. Richard knew by the tone of the letter that things had to be bad, so he immediately called her from Omaha. "All she said was 'please come home so I can see you,'" he recalled. "I got on the first train to Texas. I didn't want to leave the team, but Mama Ella meant the world to me."

The train ride to Austin seemed very long, but somewhat enjoyable. It was the first time Richard had ever been on a train, and it was a different experience for him. The train was called the *Kansas City Katie.* "To tell you the truth, I kind of felt special being able to ride that train all the way to Austin," Richard said proudly.

Richard felt something was terribly wrong with Ella and he couldn't get home quick enough. Upon his arrival in town, Richard was met at the station by his stepbrother, Lincoln. "He was real quiet and wouldn't answer any of my questions," Richard noted. "I knew then that the news from then on would be bad."

He arrived home and found Ella in bed, looking very sick. "I knew she was dying and there was nothing I could do." Apparently, she had been in very poor health for some time, but she didn't want Richard to know it. She wanted to keep it quiet so Richard wouldn't worry about her. "This was a huge blow to me," he said. "I really didn't know how much time she had left. I hung around the house for a few days trying to make her comfortable. Then it happened, just that quick—she died. I had never faced death before and it was really terrible. I cried and cried like I had lost my best friend in the whole world." He continued, "Here I was in my hometown and I felt lost, I didn't know what to do or say. I talked to my family and friends and they convinced me to go back to Nebraska after the funeral. I was sick that Mama Ella hadn't called me long before she got so bad, but it was too late now."

After the funeral, Richard spent a few days catching up on old times with his friends in town. They were glad to see him, but not any more so than he was to see them. It was both a sad and happy occasion for him. He had not wanted to return to Austin like this.

After seeing his friends he decided it was time to leave Austin, maybe this time for good. He said his goodbyes and caught the next bus back to Omaha. "I really didn't know if I could ever come back again," he said. "Life in Austin wouldn't be the same after Ella was gone."

Back in Nebraska, baseball life continued as before. Richard recalled the biggest disappointment of his short semi-pro baseball career. The Rockets were set to play a game against a player named Satchel Paige, the premier player of the Kansas City Monarchs and possibly the entire Negro League. Since the Monarchs were the major league team directly above the Rockets, this would be Richard's chance to show what he could do against the best. Paige would later be called one of the greatest baseball players ever, in any league. Although it would be many years later before he was recognized for his athletic ability by the white baseball historians, Paige was already considered the best black baseball player in the country.

Paige and his team were set to come to Omaha to play the Rockets, and Richard was priming himself for the opportunity to play against him. Paige was well known for his ability to pitch, and Richard had a great ability to hit the ball. When word of the upcoming game came down, Richard was mentally preparing himself to "Show Satchel what I had," he said. "For days I worked real hard to sharpen my skills. I put in lots of extra time just to make sure I was at my best. I had every pitcher on our team throwing pitches until their arms fell off."

The day of the game arrived. Richard got up that morning very early, even though the game wasn't until later that afternoon. To his dismay, it was raining. Hour after hour he waited it out, praying for the rain to stop, but it didn't. He finally went down to the park an hour before the scheduled game time. "I just sat there, looking at the sky, and I started crying to myself. Here was my big chance to play against the best and it wasn't going to happen. I couldn't believe this was happening to me. I never saw Satchel at all that day. Maybe if I had played him then, I would have stuck with baseball instead of football, but it wasn't meant to be.

"Later on, I decided that I was bored with baseball, it was too slow for me. After that, it was football all the way."

Chapter Five

Junior College Football

School had started at Scottsbluff, and the first day of football practice had begun. As Richard was introduced to the regular team members, Coach Putman said, "I don't know what this kid can do, but he's gonna get his shot. If he makes it, he makes it. If not, well, he got his shot."

The team gathered outside and loosened up together on the field, then all the linemen took one corner of the field, while the quarterbacks, receivers, and defensive backs huddled together in another section. Assistant coaches Bill Ostenberg and Paul Landoldt both worked with the offensive and defensive positions. Since Scottsbluff was such a small school, as were all of the schools in that junior college conference, their coaches had to work in many different areas of the game—unlike the larger Division I schools, which had assistants who specialized in one area.

Jess Pilkington, a Scottsbluff player, played both offensive and defensive tackle. Jess said, "I usually lined up at left tackle, right next to Richard. The first day I could tell how good he was and how fast he was off the ball. Richard played both offensive and defensive end," remembered Pilkington. "Once when we lined up in a game I noticed that they kept running away from our left end, probably to avoid him. I took advantage of that and made several tackles. Richard made me look good many times," he said.

The practices were pretty tough, even though it was considered small-time college football by most standards. The coaches were really rough on the new students, like Richard, who were trying to make the team. They wanted to "weed out" anyone who wasn't going to really contribute. Coaches had to be selective back then, since they usually only carried about 50 men on the team roster.

During the first day of practice, the quarterbacks threw lots of passes to all the receivers. Richard was singled out because he was new and he came from Texas. "We all heard that the boys in Texas could really play ball," Jess continued.

In a matter of minutes it was apparent that Richard possessed great speed and raw talent. Vinton Ellis, another teammate who played halfback in 1947, recalled Richard's ability to "catch anything that was thrown his way." Ellis said, "You just didn't realize how quick he was until you stood next to him on the field. He weighed about 170 pounds and could really jump. I saw him many times just reach up and grab a ball with one hand. That was tough for anyone to do."

Day after day, Richard became more familiar and involved with the Cougars team plays and strategies. He quickly absorbed their playbook and used his overall knowledge to make himself surprisingly better. Vinton recalled, "Coaches Ostenberg and Landoldt were good, tough coaches. They pushed us hard with Coach Putman running the overall program. He wanted us to win and I think he saw we had some good solid players. We were going to play some pretty good teams and we had to be mentally and physically ready."

Sometime during the first week of practice, it was obvious Richard was going to make the team. Coach Putman asked Richard about his ability to pay his tuition. Richard told him, "My mother is taking care of it, but it's hard on her."

"What if I can get you a full scholarship to school?" Putman asked.

"What exactly does that mean, Coach?"

"Well, the school picks up the tab on everything—books, tuition, food, you name it," he explained. "If this is a hardship on your mom, I would recommend it."

"I'll just have to ask her," Richard answered, knowing that this was going to be great news for Johnnie Mae.

When he got home that night, Richard couldn't restrain himself and quickly told his mother the good news. "Coach Putman said I could get a full scholarship," he said, bursting with excitement.

"You tell Coach Putman thanks. But I'm gonna pay for your schooling," she replied.

"You don't want none of it?" Richard asked curiously.

"Nope. That's real nice of him, but I feel like I need to do this myself." She continued, "Do you want me to call him?"

"No. I'll just tell him tomorrow," he said, feeling slightly dejected. After all, there was a certain honor and pride that went with being a scholarship athlete.

"Now, you don't have to tell him everything about us, just that we'd like to pay our own way, that's all," said Johnnie Mae.

"Sure, I understand," said Richard.

The next day before practice, Richard went into Coach Putman's office to give him the news. To say he was surprised was an understatement. "She doesn't want it?" he asked.

"No, Coach," he responded.

"Well, that's the way it'll be then. If something changes, you just let me know."

"Yes, sir," Richard said.

As the season got under way, it was apparent to the coaches at Scottsbluff that they had a good, solid team. Their enthusiasm was great during practices and it never seemed to drop off. Dwain Riddle, the Cougars quarterback at the time, said, "Richard brought lots of excitement to our team. His contributions were readily clear, even during practice and scrimmages. He had the ability to jump up, tip a ball that was too high, then grab it out of the air. Normally, nobody could jump like that," said Riddle.

Richard showed equal ability on both sides of the ball. Although he would later become famous for his defensive skills in the National Football League, his offensive prowess was just as amazing. Jess Pilkington said, "We didn't play with facemasks back then, but we never really thought about it one way or another. They would throw Richard a ball when he was on offense and he would run with reckless abandon down the field, just daring someone to tackle him. Man, was he fast!"

It was not uncommon for student athletes to have academic or other related problems at a major university and go back to a junior college for a year or two. Richard recalled one student who attended the University of Nebraska and had played on the Cornhusker football team. "This kid played the same position I did, wide receiver. He had some type of grade problems at Nebraska and he flunked out. The next thing I know, he's trying out for my position on the Scottsbluff team. Coach Putman encouraged the competition, and I really didn't have much to say about it."

Richard said, "This white kid was really a tough competitor. He had come from a big school and he felt he could run the show at Scottsbluff. From the first day, he was a big problem for me. I knew he was a good, solid player, but I also knew I was better than he was. I was on the field several times in the huddle with the team when this kid would run up to me and tell me to go to the sidelines. He always said the coach wanted to see me. I'd run over to Coach Putman and he'd just stand there, staring at me."

"Richard, what the hell are you doing over here?" Putman would say.

"I thought you wanted to see me, Coach," Richard asked.

"No. I want you to get back in there and show me something," he replied.

Richard knew that the kid had tricked him, but he didn't want to show he couldn't handle it, so he'd play it cool. He would run back onto the field and tell the kid that one of the assistant coaches wanted to see him instead. "It worked pretty well," he noted.

Finally, Coach Putman realized that this kid was the only one on the team giving Richard a tough time. He asked Richard, "Listen, son, if that kid's causing you problems you just let me know and I'll handle it."

"Don't worry, Coach. I can take care of it," he answered.

Take care of it he did. Richard made the starting team playing both the offensive and defensive end positions. He continued as a starter the entire season and played a dramatic role in most of their games. His starting status was a great reward for all the mental anguish the other kid had given him. Also, all of the other players on the team saw how he handled the adversity, and this in turn got him more respect, especially for a freshman.

The Scottsbluff Cougars played games in Nebraska, Wyoming, Colorado, and South Dakota. Everywhere they played, Richard was one of the best performers on the gridiron. Pilkington recalled playing a game in Laramie, Wyoming, which the Cougars lost 19-6. "It was one of the few places where we heard any racial remarks directed toward him. I don't really recall any other blacks playing on the opposing teams, but they had some Mexican players, just like we did, but no blacks," said Pilkington. "They lit into Richard real hard, but it really didn't bother him. I guess he had heard it all before down in Texas. And I think it made him play harder, just to prove them wrong."

"He was faster than anyone on any of the other teams too. It was that simple," noted Dwain Riddle. "They didn't have anything or anyone to compete with him. I think back to some of those games and laugh to myself. We had a great player in our midst."

"I don't really think the coaches at Scottsbluff realized what they had on their hands back then," Pilkington recalled. "He was something else. I sure would have liked to have seen all those guys on his high school team in Austin."

During one game, Richard was playing defensive end and the opposing team threw a pass in his area of the field. "Richard just batted the ball up in the air, grabbed it, then ran 50 yards in for the score. He made it look real easy," Pilkington said.

Most of the games at the junior college level were very competitive, just like they were on the major college campuses around the country. Richard recalled one instance in a game that has been with him for more than 50 years. "We were playing an away game against a tough opponent. I remember that Johnnie Mae and my stepfather, Ronald Moore, were at the game. I caught a pass and was running as hard as I could downfield and I got forced out of bounds. The next thing I know, I'm slipping on the sidelines and all of a sudden I hit the ground hard, sliding across the edge of the dirt and grass area. When I stop sliding, I'm halfway under the fence that surrounds the field and I'm looking up at several spectators that have run down from their seats."

Richard continued his recollection. "I'm trying to get up when this man starts kicking me and cussing me. He wasn't hurting me at all, since I had on full pads, but he just keeps on kicking me while I'm down. I look up and some of my teammates are running toward me, yelling at him all the way.

"Suddenly," he said, "I look behind the man and I see my stepdad, Ronald, standing next to the guy and pointing a pistol at him. Ronald always carried a pistol since he and my mom worked the tavern. Well, everybody kind of jumps back when they see the pistol being waved around. Ronald taps the guy on the arm and says, 'You kick him again and I'll blow your damn head off!' Well, I finally get to my feet about this time and my teammates are pulling me away from the guy."

The crowd was buzzing with the commotion and the game was stopped. Richard could picture it well. "I then see the guy's wife or girlfriend grab him by the arm and start pulling him away. Then I see that the guy's shaking all over and he can't stop shaking. I'm kind of laughing to myself about now and then I start thinking, what if he really shoots him? I'm pretty sure the guy called me nigger, but to tell you the truth I was so startled it was hard to remember."

The following week the president of the opposing school sent Coach Putman a letter apologizing for the incident. Richard said, "Coach Putman called me into his office and read the letter to me. I thought that was real nice of that school to send the letter."

When asked about the fact that Ronald pulled a pistol and whether he would have used it, Richard said, "I think maybe he would have, if he had kicked me again. To tell you the truth, it was kind of funny. I could have easily grabbed the guy and beat him up a little, but I didn't. I know that the cops came up later and asked who pulled a gun and we all just said we didn't know. I'm sure that guy got the worst of the deal. He looked real bad as his wife pulled him away." He concluded, "I heard about that incident the rest of the year. All the guys on my team kept asking me if Ronald might shoot them if things got rough in practice. They all laughed about it."

Vinton Ellis said, "Yeah, that's all true. Plus, a lot of other funny things happened that I can't mention. But what I recall most about Richard was that he loved playing defense so he could really hit someone. He just would tee off and level them. Plus, he was a great individual. It was amazing to me: here he was the only black guy on the team and he fit in just perfect. He was a good person to be around."

In the 1940s and 1950s football players never lifted weights, since they thought it would make them muscle-bound and slow. Ellis recalled, "I remember Night Train being in our locker room. What a physique he had. He put most of us to shame in that respect. During one game I recall him playing defensive end and he constantly yelled at the opposing quarterback, 'Hey, just throw it over here, this black on me won't rub off!' I guess he was going to hit the guy real hard and prove a point. And he usually did."

Richard recalled a game against one of the two teams that beat them that year, Norfolk, Nebraska. "We lost that one by a score of 12-8. But I know we got cheated out of it by the referees. I scored the first three times I touched the ball, but each time the touchdown was called back for nitpicking calls, you know, calls that could easily go either way. Even Coach Putman ran onto the field a few times during that game and threatened to fight each referee. He was that mad. All the refs used some 'trickeration' against us that day."

As the game went on, things didn't improve. He noted in particular a pass play at the very end of the game that could have changed the outcome. "I caught a pass on our own 10-yard line and started zig zagging across the field. If I score, we probably win the game. I'm closing on the other goal line when a guy makes a good tackle on me about the 10-yard line."

The events surrounding the game got stranger. "As I'm lying on the ground after the tackle I distinctly remember hearing the whistle. Suddenly, this other player strips the ball from me and starts running with it. All our guys were yelling at the ref, 'Stop the clock!' But they never did. The play was over, but the clock kept running and we lost the game. It was a shame, really."

Moments after the game the players were furious. Richard remembers running after one of the refs and yelling, "I'm gonna kick your ass!" Two of Richard's players grabbed him and held him back.

The commotion about the poor officiating was even clear to the opposing spectators. As the Scottsbluff team dejectedly walked off the field Richard heard one of the other team's fans yell, "Hell, that little blackie can really run, but you guys stole the game from those kids!"

A few days after that game, another letter came to Scottsbluff Junior College. "The president of that school also apologized to our school president. Apparently, some of their own fans complained about the refereeing so much they felt bad about it. All I know is, we got cheated real bad," he said.

Dwain Riddle recalled, "Some of those games were really wild. But Richard was a little wild too, in a funny way. He would yell at me during a game, 'Hey, Dwain, you white boy, just hang it out there, I'll get it.' He didn't mean anything by the white boy remark, he just wanted me to throw it deep so he could make a spectacular catch. I really liked him a lot as a person, just as much as a player. You also might think that him being the only black in town might cause some problems, but it didn't happen. He was well respected and received by the community."

Richard later said, "I traveled all across the country and I never met any better folks than the fine people across Nebraska. They treated me real nice. I would call them the salt of the earth. I remember several of them telling me that if I ever got hungry, 'Just come by the house and eat what you want. The fridge is always open.' You can't go many places in this country and be treated like that."

"He wasn't a show off by any means," Riddle said. "He just wanted to play ball. After seeing what he could do, I wasn't sur-prised he made it into the NFL or the Hall of Fame. There couldn't be too many guys around with his natural ability."

Following World War II, many of the men returned from duty and went to college. Most of those men were ages 23-25 and had lots of maturity compared to the normal junior college kid. Jess Pilkington remembered, "You would think these older guys would try to intimidate us with their experience and age. In some cases, they did just that, but not to Richard Lane. They all seemed to give him more respect than normal—respect that was greater than his age would probably deserve at first glance."

Richard recalled his team's record that year (1947) at Scottsbluff. "It was 5-2-1. We scored a total of 125 points to our opponents' 57. I had some great teammates with me and believe me, they worked their butts off during the entire season. Prior to the season opener, all the players got together and pledged to make 1947 one of the best in school history. I'm not sure how we compared to all those other years, but I know we did our best." He also noted, "I was voted junior college all-American in 1947. I felt very fortunate about that honor.

"Several people over the years asked me about any racial conflicts I had in Scottsbluff, since there weren't any blacks on the team roster," Richard continued. "Racial problems never came up at all. I couldn't have been treated better, on or off the field. On weekends or after games, I was always invited to every function. The other players' parents always included me in any of their activities or parties."

Richard developed a close relationship with a student who wasn't on the football team. His name was Richard Fink. "Richard Fink was a real smart kid and he helped me through my tough classes. His mother was very caring toward all the athletes in school and she helped arrange for special tutoring classes for us. I'm not sure she ever got the appreciation she really deserved. She treated me very well."

Richard recalled some of the other activities Mrs. Fink set up. "She operated a club we referred to as the Bearcat Club. All the students knew that they could come to the club anytime they wanted and have some fun. It consisted of organized ping-pong games and pool tournaments. It doesn't sound like much now, but back then it was lots of fun. She was a mother for all the students whose real parents weren't near the school."

After Richard became more comfortable with the school, he finally agreed to go out with one of the cheerleaders for the football team, a very cute white girl. She had asked him out several times, but he had felt uneasy with the situation. Here he was, the only black at Scottsbluff Junior College, who got along well with everyone he met in town. But dating a white girl might be pushing the boundaries. He confided in a few teammates about it and they advised him to take her out.

Richard recalled the circumstances surrounding their date. "She wanted to go up to a place near school called 'The Bluff.'

It was a mountain outside of town and really it was the only mountain anywhere around town. Scottsbluff was really flat, so it wasn't too hard to name this place 'The Bluff.'

"Well, she really liked me a lot and I think she wanted to impress me with some of her athletic ability, since I was on the football team and all. It was real cold and snowing that day so she wanted to take me skiing. I figured what the heck, I can play basketball, football or whatever, I'm sure I can ski too. How hard could that be?"

Richard had no idea what lay ahead for him. They arrived at The Bluff and were greeted by many friends from town. Everyone was putting on skis and having a great time laughing and talking about how good they were at downhill skiing. Richard laced up a pair of ski boots "which felt really strange," he noted. "The next thing I know, I'm standing on the edge of a steep hill looking down, but I still didn't realize my mistake until a few seconds later."

As Richard gained speed going downhill he realized how dangerous skiing was and how little his athletic prowess would help him. "Within two or three seconds I was totally out of control. The bad thing was, I couldn't grab hold of anything. I knew for sure this was my last day on earth or at the very least I would break my neck." After several hard crashes across the small mountain, Richard felt that bravery wasn't the way to pursue this activity. He jerked off his skis and ski boots, and he didn't care who saw him or what they thought. "I was just glad not to be crippled," he said.

His date was laughing hard at his expense, until she realized the terror on his face. "If I had known you were going to have such a hard time out here, I never would have suggested it," she said to him, all the while trying to suppress a laugh.

"Don't you worry about it," he responded. "I'm just glad it's over."

Richard recalled other girls. "Several times during the school year I was interested in dating some of the attractive Nebraska farm girls and a few times they even asked me out. But I know what problems racial strife can cause and I didn't want any of their fathers looking for me later. My skin color hadn't been an issue since I arrived in town and I didn't want it to surface now. So, I usually just played it safe and was kind of low-key about it."

In and around Scottsbluff the gambling joints and some houses of "ill repute" were making their way into the population. Richard had learned many of the street hustler con moves in his days in Austin, most notably street craps, pool, and card games. "I was real good at it," he noted. "It wasn't an honest living, but when you had to have some quick money that was the way to make it."

With this type of easy money to be had, it was so tempting to do it full time, instead of studying in school or working hard at athletics. "I fit in real good with those types, but Mama Ella didn't raise me to be a street hustler. You wouldn't believe the temptation it was to just live the hustler's life. I'm sure that was part of the reason my grades in class weren't too good. I spent too much time away from school," he added.

Somewhere in this time period Richard found out that his mother, Johnnie Mae, was working the streets again. "I was really upset with this news. For years and years that's all I ever heard about her, then she moves to Nebraska and I think it's over. I had a belly full of this long before. So, I confront her with it and she won't say anything at all. Then, I know it's true." He concluded, "I didn't want to be in the same town with her again with this going on around me. I got mad at her and totally rebelled. I quit school and decided to join the military. Besides, I thought that would be a good way to get my education paid for later on."

Chapter Six

Life in the Army

Throughout Richard's early life he had always been interested in planes and learning how to fly. He had excellent eyesight and was in perfect health. Plus, at that time, his one year of college could enable him to enter officer school in some branch of the military. After he finally decided to leave Scottsbluff, he wanted his first try at military life to be with the air force.

"I just walked into the nearest air force recruiting office and told them point-blank that I wanted to join up and fly planes. I told them about my year of junior college and I had my grades ready for the recruiter." But, he added, "As usual, what you want, you can't have. The military was very segregated then and the air force had totally white and black outfits, and many units were separate from each other. The recruiter told me that the pilot squadrons were totally full, since the war was just over and they had lots of good pilots left who wanted to stay in the service."

Richard recalled standing in the recruiter's office, "totally dejected." He said, "But then the guy gave me some good news. He said to me, 'Listen son, the army has lots of excellent officers and pilots. You should consider them also.' He wrote down the address of the army recruiter and I immediately started walking out the door. I had made up my mind to join the military and if the srmy had some pilots, I'd just try for that instead."

Upon his arrival at the army recruiter, Richard was told he indeed had a chance to fly. He remembers them saying something like, "The sky's the limit for young men." Richard continued with his military recollections. "I filled out all the necessary papers and they swore me in. It was a proud moment for me, and looking back on it years later, it was one of the best things I could have done. I signed up for three years, but wound up doing a four-year stint. The extra year I volunteered to stay in because the army requested it. It really developed my character and taught me about being a good American and citizen."

Basic training took place at Fort Knox, Kentucky, in the dead of winter in 1948. "It was thirteen weeks of hard manual labor," he said. "Every minute of every day was spent under the watchful eye of the drill sergeant. A person that really wanted to see us suffer," he added. "But I was young, tough, and determined. I knew I'd make it through the training period, and I was determined to make it to Officer Candidate School so I could learn how to fly."

Richard was assigned to the 84th Tank Battalion, Army Infantry. "A fine group of guys to work with," he said. "Our biggest problem was heat in the classrooms. There wasn't any! I always wondered why they couldn't heat our buildings in the dead of winter. Man, it seemed like I was always cold." He shivered at the memory.

"Revilee was at 4:00 A.M. every day," he said. "I was tough and all, but getting up at 4:00 wasn't my idea of fun. It seemed like all we did was run, do pushups and situps, and clean the barracks. Then, the rest of the day was taken up with marching, studying, and anything else the drill sergeant could think of. As I look back on it, I think it was great for me, but I wouldn't want to do it forever."

At the earliest possible time, Richard went to the officer's building and signed up for Officer Candidate School. He told them again he wanted to fly planes and "the quicker the better," he said. He knew his single year of college wasn't much, but at that time one year of advanced education was all it took to be eligible for the school. "I knew deep down it would be a long shot with my limited college, but I wanted to fly so bad I had to give it a chance," Richard said.

The weeks passed by and Richard's dreams of flying seemed to fade away like the planes that peeled off the tarmac and into the sky. One day Richard was in the sports complex when some-one pointed out the bulletin board that listed all the army sports programs, which included football, basketball, and baseball. Each sport had a certain day for team tryouts, and several of Richard's fellow recruits decided to try them all.

Fort Knox was under the command of General Maddox in 1948, but the person who oversaw the sports programs for the army base was a black woman named Mrs. Collier. "She was a rough, tough lady who knew her sports," Richard recalled. "I was as surprised as anyone else when she walked out to meet us for the football team tryouts. I had never been around any women that knew anything about the sport. But, I'll tell you what, not only did she know football, she would get down in a stance with us and work on our fundamentals."

During his hitch in the service, Richard met a female recruit named Geraldine Dandridge. Geraldine was a member of the WAC, or the Women's Auxiliary Corps. They dated for several months and Geraldine became pregnant. They married a short time later, and from the outset Geraldine accused Richard of marrying her only because she was pregnant. But, Richard said, "I really loved her, a lot. I tried real hard to convince her of that, but I'm not sure she ever believed me."

A few months later Geraldine had a miscarriage and lost the baby. "She was really devastated," Richard said. "Little did I know that it would be the first of several miscarriages for her." Richard soon discovered that Geraldine was an alcoholic, a fact that totally caught him by surprise. "All the times we were together I never saw it. She drank, all right, but never so much I would have suspected that she was addicted to the booze. She was just like her father all along. It really broke my heart."

Over the next eleven years, their married life was engulfed in turmoil and it always seemed to center around her drinking problem. "I finally learned that all my extra money I left around the house was being spent on alcohol. It would disappear a lit-tle at a time and I never suspected it was happening like that," he said. Year after year they struggled to keep their marriage intact. "Several times I sent her back to her folks home in Richmond, Virginia. They were very supportive of her and really loved her, but it didn't work. As soon as she got alone, the drinking just started over. I grew up with my mother having this problem and it just started eating away at me again. Here I was married to Geraldine and I was fighting another uphill battle, a battle I was losing."

Geraldine was able to hold down good jobs throughout their marriage and in each job she maintained herself in a responsible way, but the alcohol was always lurking in the background. "One time she even got a good job at a Methodist church. Those church people were real nice to her and they really liked her, but the booze just kept her totally messed up. She would usually leave the church to go do some errands and then she'd just wind up drunk at home or in some bar."

As Richard's personal life in the army continued to spiral downwards, his athletic life was going in another direction. He was making fast friends with some of the other recruits like Billy Anderson, Eule McBride, and Tommy Mason, all great athletes in their own right. "These guys were truly outstanding ball players in every respect," Richard said. "We all made the army basketball team at the same time. I thought I was a great hoops player until I got around those guys. They all could really 'look off' an opponent and make a good pass going up and down the floor."

Most of the army basketball competition was between the different services, just as the football competition was at that time. They would play each of the teams in the navy, marine, and air force academies. "Most of the teams were fairly matched, but some years there would be big lopsided games just as there would be in any university athletics competition. The guys on our teams were good solid athletes, and we usually blended well together on the court."

"Eule McBride is still the best all-around basketball player I ever saw at any level. That guy could outdribble anyone. I usually played the center position where I could dunk the ball, but he seemed to be able to jump even higher than I could," said Richard with a grin. "He was extremely fast and unbelievably coordinated on the court. When they would stop him from driving inside, he would just stop at the top of the key and hit a long jumper. He was comfortable with any shot on the floor. He was one of the few guys I had trouble covering in our practices."

Segregation was a way of life even in the army. Richard's tank battalion was primarily black, with some whites and other minorities included. The issue of race didn't really come up until Richard tried to move up through the ranks. "On the surface they wanted you to succeed and that's what they told everyone. But in reality, being black might have been a mark against you. There had to be some unwritten rule on the number of minority men they would promote within the army. It's something I really don't like discussing, even today," he said. "But I've noticed over the last 25 years or so, they've really made great strides in this area. I once made an application to get into Army Language School, but supposedly my limited education kept me from getting into their classes. I've always wondered if it was my race that prohibited me. I was also told that my application to Officer Candidate School had been approved, but for some reason the orders were later canceled."

The highest rank Richard achieved was that of corporal. "To tell you the truth, that was as high as I wanted to go. There was way too much politics in it and the higher you went, the worse it got." He continued, "I was responsible for filling out the daily reports on each man in our unit. If they were sick, I reported it to the sergeant. After I did that each day, I had lots of time to do my other duties and then I practiced whatever sports I was engaged in at that time."

Richard was also responsible for driving the communications jeep for the lieutenant. "I just drove him around the base during whatever maneuvers we were doing that day and that was my total job. I'll never forget we almost got killed one day on the base at Fort Ord, California. Our tank battalion was set up to shoot their 88-millimeter rounds at a nearby hill, and the lieutenant wanted to get a good look at the action. He directed me to drive up to the top of the next hill to watch them fire.

"Well, there was one big problem, they were shooting at our hill instead. As we drove up the hill the rounds started hitting all around us. I don't know who jumped out of the jeep faster, but after we hit the ground I know I was outrunning him back down the hill. I was scared then, but later on I thought it was really funny. The guys in the unit never let us forget that one," said Richard, laughing at the memory.

While continuing his stint at Fort Ord, Richard worked on his football and basketball careers, while returning to an old one, baseball. His time with the Omaha Rockets served him well, and his baseball skills were above average at this level. "I really liked pitching since I could control the game," he recalled, "but my best position was the outfield, where I could run down any fly balls they hit my way."

Life with Geraldine was continuing at a slow pace and her drinking problems followed them to California. "I hoped the change would work for her, but nothing slowed her down in that respect," he noted. "I could tell that my friends knew she was a drunk, but they did their best to avoid any confrontations with her or me. I still loved her greatly, but it was just killing me to see her that way all the time. Every time I left town and then returned home, I was confronted with a huge liquor bill from the local liquor store. I found out she was having huge parties when I was gone."

Other than his problems with Geraldine, life at Fort Ord was great. It really brightened up when someone told Richard he could make $10 a game if he could make the local semi-pro football team that played on the weekends. The Santa Cruz, California, Seahawks were a solid semi-pro team, and getting paid for hitting people was right up his alley. "We played some good teams in and around Santa Cruz and I loved every minute of it," he said. "Besides, Geraldine was keeping a big scrapbook on me which kept track of all my football and basketball accomplishments. I really had no idea that the scrapbook would come in handy later when I tried to make the Los Angeles Rams team."

Chapter Seven

Making the Big Leagues

As his army time drew to a close, Richard was faced with the realization that he had to get a real job outside the military. He had spoken to a few friends in Los Angeles who advised him that a company in town called North American Aircraft was looking for ex-military men. Richard also wanted to stay in L.A. since Geraldine had a good job with the city. She had made some good strides toward controlling her drinking problem, and now would not be a good time to move.

The day Richard applied at North American Aircraft, he was pleased to find out that the company had a basketball team. A player of his caliber would be welcomed into their midst. He told them he was leaving the army within a few weeks and he made the application right on the spot. "This job looked real good to me at first, and what I liked most about it was it gave me the chance to stay in shape, just in case I could get a place on some ball club," he said.

"Well, things didn't work out too good for me. I had only been at the company a few months, but the job was really boring and I didn't get the pay I felt I deserved. They had me stacking big sheets of oil-covered metal. It was a terrible job. I thought I should be doing something better."

In the area of athletics, Richard continued to excel. "We continued to play some hoops around town against other teams and we did pretty well. Little did I know that things were really going to change for me real soon.

"While I played basketball at North American, I didn't know that some college scout had watched one of our games and had later asked some questions about me. This guy walks up to me one night and says he's real impressed with my ball handling ability and he wanted to know about my education. Well, I told him I only had one year of junior college ball and I basically had three years' eligibility left in college. He was real excited."

A short time later the scout contacted Richard again after another company game. This time he came prepared with an offer—a full scholarship to Loyola Marymount College to play basketball.

"I would start immediately for the varsity?" Richard wondered.

"Probably so. As long as the head coach agrees with me," he answered.

"Man, and I get everything paid for too."

"That's right," the scout responded.

"Well, you just tell me when to show up and I'll be there," Richard said.

"Come into the athletic office in three weeks, when the head coach returns."

"I'll be there."

A short time later, Richard learned from an old army buddy, Gabby Simms, that Simms had been drafted by the Los Angeles Rams as a backup quarterback. Simms would be behind Norm Van Brocklin and Bob Waterfield on the depth chart. Simms told Richard that several members of the Rams team worked out daily at a city park in L.A. "He knew what I could do and told me to write a letter to the head coach and then he'd introduce me to the veterans during an informal workout. So, I sent the letter to the Rams office and the next day I met with Gabby and his buddies in the park. I didn't know it then, but the Rams' scout, Eddie Kotel, had already seen me play in the army and he put in a good word for me also."

During that first meeting all the Rams players, plus Richard, were working out and running wind sprints in a city park in Los Angeles. "You've got to understand," he added. "I had no intention of not going back to college. That was a big deal to me. Especially Loyola Marymount. Man, that was a good school."

As the workout progressed, it was apparent that Richard was just as good at football as any of the veteran players. One of them remarked, "Man, you're fast! Gabby said you played some army ball?"

"Sure thing," Richard responded.

"You show the coaches what you've got and it won't be no problem making the team."

"I told you boys I knew what I was talking about," Simms piped in. "This dude can play all right."

Toward the end of the workout they all agreed to run wind sprints against each other, just to settle once and for all who was the fastest. "I was quick, but Woodley Lewis, whom I had met at the Rams office, was just as fast as I was," Richard said. "I knew I had to be at my best."

"How far we going?" Gabby said.

"How about a hundred yards?" Richard asked the group.

"Sounds good to me," one of them answered.

As they all lined up near the end of the grass in the park clearing, they peered at each other, knowing someone would walk away with bragging rights. "How about to that tree?" Gabby said as he pointed across the field.

"Looks about a hundred to me," Richard yelled back.

"When I say go, we go," Gabby yelled.

"Don't wait on me."

An instant later Gabby yelled "go" and the race started. As they flew past several onlookers, people stared at them, not knowing what was going on but still marveling at the speed of the men. In about ten seconds, Richard and Woodley Lewis reached the particular tree at the end of the clearing a few yards ahead of the others.

Finally, Lewis chimed in with the remark, "Hell, I thought you boys could run."

"You want to do it again?" Richard asked them.

"You're on, buddy. Yell when you're ready," Lewis said.

As they lined up again, Gabby had a much more determined look on his face. But the outcome was still the same. Richard and Lewis won by several yards. "Is that fast enough for you?" Richard asked.

"Hell, yeah. Dammit man, you're quick," Lewis said. "I guess all that military and college ball did you some good."

"Only one year of junior college. The rest was in the army," Richard told him.

"What was your college team?"

"Scottsbluff. In Nebraska."

"Never heard of it. A big school?" he asked.

"Nope. Small junior college, but it was a good one."

Gabby butted into their conversation. "You guys want to meet here tomorrow? Dick Lane will show you boys how to catch some balls one-handed too."

Richard smiled as he heard this invitation, before he finally responded, "You bring the ball. I'll show you."

The next day was more of the same, except this time Richard put on a display of great ball-catching ability. Gabby threw passes and "We ran routes until our legs gave out," Richard said. "He could throw the ball pretty good and I was making one-handed catches all over the place." Richard felt confident about his chances with the Rams and made a comment about his basketball abilities. "You guys ever play any hoops? I'm better at that."

"I don't care about any damn hoops," Gabby said pointedly. "If I get you a tryout with the Rams, I don't want you to flake out on me."

"What's that mean?"

"You need to show up and do what they say, that's what."

"Believe me, you get me the chance and I'll show up all right," Richard said enthusiastically.

Gabby continued, "Just call the front office in ten days. I know your letter got to Coach Stydahar."

"Thanks, Gabby," Richard remarked, knowing full well this was a great chance. "I really appreciate your help."

"Listen, if you can play anything like you can run and catch, they'll be happy to see you," Lewis blurted out.

"Don't worry, just get me in the door with a fair shot."

Richard remembered how fast it all happened. "One minute I'm going back to college, then the next I'm walking on with the defending world champion Rams. College took an immediate back seat."

During these early times in Los Angeles, Geraldine had applied for and later received a job with the city. It was a good paying job with great benefits, and it seemed to be the right time for her to try and beat her drinking problem. She and Richard remained very close personally and they even talked about trying to have kids again, even with her physical problems, which caused the prior miscarriages. All in all, things were looking up for the couple.

The weeks passed and Richard made good time with his tough workout schedule. He met several of the Rams players on a regular basis and even got to meet some of the Cleveland Browns players who lived in Los Angeles in the off-season. They all took to his friendly personality and his hard work ethic. He hadn't made the team yet, but he was treated like an equal while he was among the NFL veterans. Although they didn't verbalize it at the time, many of the veterans knew Richard could make the team, if he was given a fair chance to do so.

The Los Angeles Rams complex was a simple but effective football facility in 1952. Being the defending NFL champions carried weight and attached an honor to each member of the team. Years later, most NFL observers would comment that the players of those eras could simply play ball better and were much tougher than the players of today. In many respects, this was a valid statement. The players of the 1950s and 1960s were surely not compensated enough for their sacrifices. There were no gigantic signing bonuses and the yearly wages were in the thousands of dollars, even for the hard-nosed veterans who had put it all on the line for their respective teams.

The league of the 1950s consisted mostly of white ball players with a few black men sprinkled into each squad. Although racism was not a big issue on the teams, it existed nonetheless, just as it did in everyday society. So, with this background, it was very difficult for any black athlete to make a "white roster" on a pro football team, and it was extremely hard for the same black player to make it into the starting lineup.

Excitement was in the air as the defending world champions walked through the Rams' front doors in the late summer of 1952 to start their yearly training camp. Being the champs was a twofold experience. First, all the other teams wanted a piece of the champs, and each player had to play harder to keep the team at that high level. Second, the title of world champs carried a large banner in itself. It meant instant stardom and recognition within NFL circles.

The first day of a long training camp session was a time for each man to assess his position skills and overall conditioning. Also, each man was out to retain his job or to take another man's place on the team roster. When Richard was introduced that first day, several of the men had already met him through the prior weeks of workouts in the city park. To some, he was just another rookie who had to "make the grade or hit the road."

"I kind of got the cold shoulder from some of the players," he remembered. "But that was all right. Woodley Lewis and Gabby had told me plenty already. I knew what was coming. But the funny thing was, even though I had spent all that time working out with them, I was still real nervous. I couldn't eat or sleep the night before and I had major butterflies!"

All of the coaches came into the locker room and talked to each player briefly. Some of the veterans received more personal treatment from the coaches, and as Richard noted, "That was to be expected." All of the players were weighed in front of each other and they kidded certain players who were overweight. In Richard's case, a few of them made comments about him being too small for "big time football." Richard told them, "If you can catch me, then you can worry about how small I am."

The head coach of the Rams was Joe Stydahar, a hard-nosed competitor that knew the game inside and out. Stydahar was well respected throughout the league by both the players and the other coaches. "I knew I had my chance at making the team," Richard recalled. "Stydahar wanted the best and I had to perform, just like everyone else, but he was extremely fair-minded."

The man who coached the tight ends was Red Hickey—a no-nonsense man who didn't cut anybody much slack, especially a rookie like Richard Lane who had come into their midst as a walk-on player with limited prior playing experience. Hickey made it clear that Lane wasn't at the top of his list of favorite players. "Hickey really jumped on me from the get go," Richard said. "He said to me 'Lane, you're too damn small to be playing at this level. We already have some great receivers on this team and no slots left to fill in.'"

Richard responded with, "Well, I can play defense just as good if not better than offense anyway."

After the greetings by all the players and coaches, they took the field for some loosening up exercises and did a brief run through some of the basic drills. Afterwards, Stydahar walked up to Richard and asked for any news clippings or articles he had from either junior college or army football. Richard told him he would bring them to him the next day. It was at this time that Richard found out that the Rams scout, Eddie Kotel, had already passed on a good word about Richard's playing ability, and it was apparent that Coach Stydahar just wanted to see some general clippings from the games.

The first day of full practice was a bad experience for Richard. He was still very nervous and hadn't been able to eat or sleep well. He knew everyone was waiting for him to make a mistake, and it wasn't too long before it happened. Richard knew from his talk with Red Hickey that his chance at wide receiver wasn't too good, but he didn't care. "I really wanted to play defense anyway, just to show them I could cover anybody on the field. And I wanted to show them that I could really hit," he said.

On top of all his usual problems trying to make the team, the local media coverage was better than normal because these were the defending champions. "I never had anyone come up to me like those boys did," he recalled. "Every time I walked off the practice field they were asking me questions. I wasn't used to that treatment, that's for sure. Every reporter kept saying that my chances of making the team were horrible. After a while of listening to that, I began to think they might be right. It worked on my mind."

At the outset of practice, Richard caught several passes along with the starting offensive ends, but he realized they were just letting him go through the motions. He was making good catches and was running good solid routes, but "I knew they really didn't have me in mind for their offensive plans."

Finally, at the end of practice, they switched him to defensive back and he ran some plays with the rest of the defense. He thought he was doing pretty good until they made all the defensive backs line up against the tackling dummies which were on heavy sleds. Richard heard the whistle and he hit the dummies as hard as he could. The whistle sounded again, and again he slammed into the sled. Then, it happened. He fainted. When he awoke, his teammates were standing over him, helping him up and pouring water on his head.

After he regained his senses, he knew the worst was coming, a tongue lashing from Coach Hickey. He didn't have to wait very long. "Hickey walked over to me and said, 'Son, you better get your act together. You do that tomorrow and you're out of here.'" Richard continued, "He turned and walked off, knowing he held the hammer on me. I knew my cat of nine lives was down to one. Between the heat, the fact I hadn't eaten or slept right in two days, and the pressure I put on myself, I just collapsed."

That night at home Richard sat alone, very depressed, knowing he couldn't have done much worse. He displayed his skills on offense, but defense was going to be his only shot at making it, since the offense was already ripe with solid receivers. Geraldine came home from work and immediately saw him in a dejected state. She tried to comfort him in some way. "Honey, tomorrow will be different, you wait and see," she said.

"It better be, because I won't be around for a third chance."

Geraldine sat beside him on the couch and rested her head on his big shoulders. "I've got faith in you. You've never let me down so far." Richard just leaned against her, not uttering a word.

The next day arrived, and as Richard walked into the Rams complex he knew he'd be shown the door if he didn't perform. It would be the first time in his football career he would have failed. He decided then and there that this would be different. "I made up my mind to kick some butt. I might not make the team, but they'd remember me hitting someone."

On top of all his mental anguish with his first day failures, Geraldine was drinking again. The night before, he could smell liquor on her breath. But, in his state of mind, he hadn't argued with her about it. Richard was worried about her and had told

her to seek professional help. He would do whatever was needed for her to beat this addiction. But his speech had fallen on
deaf ears. "Every time I saw her drunk or coming back into the
house after being out bar hopping, it just killed me," he said. "I
went out at night looking for her. It usually wasn't hard locating
her. This had been going on for five years and we weren't getting any closer to solving the problem. It was very clear to me
that I couldn't do it by myself, no matter how hard I tried."

Richard arranged for Geraldine to visit her relatives again,
as she had done before, and again he called them before she
arrived, to tell them that Geraldine's problem continued. He
begged them to do whatever they could to help her. They agreed
to take her in again, but they also knew it was an uphill battle.
Richard discussed the options they had for her treatment, but if
she wouldn't voluntarily seek help, the end of the road would
come sooner than they wanted.

As Richard continued his walk through the Rams complex,
he knew his career was at his fingertips. He was focused and
completely ready. As practice started he was aware that several
of his Rams training partners from the prior weeks were closely
watching his every move. He started out on offense again. The
quarterbacks threw several short passes to him and he immediately made his presence known by "blowing past" the defensive
backs. "I was running like a wild man," he said. "I caught everything they threw at me. I made several one-handed catches too.
I was making quick cuts across the field and changing speeds as
I ran through the secondary. I was really working at my best."

Then the defensive coaches asked him to run some defensive plays. "At that point, I just wanted to hit someone. I was
ready to lay the lumber to some of their receivers." They set up
several different offensive schemes, and on each snap Richard
covered his designated man without a hitch. In fact, he made it
look easy as he cut them off on the line of scrimmage or batted
down any passes thrown his direction. "Man, it was working just
like clockwork. I made some great tackles and on a few of the
plays where my receiver had me beat, I just turned on the speed
and made up the ground, making a good play on the ball. I was
really impressing them all."

As practice wound down to a close, the coaches made the offensive and defensive squads line up across the goal line to run sprints. The day before, Richard hadn't been able to do this, having collapsed during the tackling drills. Today would be different. "I still had lots of energy left at the end of the practice," he noted. "Woodley Lewis and Bob Boyd were fast guys, but not faster than me. It was great to run against them." In less than 10 seconds, the race was over and Richard had beaten them all. The coaches were kind of stunned and ordered them to run it again. They lined up and did it again, with the same result. "Woodley and Gabby Simms knew what was coming, but not the other guys. I was proud of my performance that day. Over the next few days we continued to sprint and sometimes Woodley or Bob would beat me or we'd reach the goal line together. They were great runners."

A few days later the scrimmages were intensifying as the coaches tried to cut the weak players from the roster. But Richard's assault on them never relented. As Richard continued to impress on defense, they just kept throwing passes at him and kept running plays his direction. "They really wanted to see my stuff," he remembered. "It would make good headlines to have a walk-on player make the team."

Once, "Deacon" Dan Tyler lined up at running back as Richard stood at the defensive end position. "Deacon Dan was fast and tough. He weighed about 220 pounds. I knew he was gonna try to run over my butt." An instant later, the play was in motion, with Deacon Tyler running full steam at Richard's end position. And, just as fast, the play was over, as Richard made a good solid tackle. All of the players on offense were impressed. Richard noted, "It was nothing fancy, just a good solid tackle."

Deacon Tyler jumped up and stood right in Richard's face. "Good tackle, man. Can you do it again?"

"You get them to run it over this way again, I'll be standing here."

As the practice continued, the intensity increased. The offense was really putting some good pressure on the defensive unit. Richard continued to make good tackles all across the field. A couple of series later, Deacon Tyler came around end again, right into Richard, who made another clean tackle. Across the field, the coaches were realizing the diamond in the rough they had found in this walk-on player. They ordered another end sweep by the offense. This time, an offensive tackle hit Richard as he came up to make the play. Richard flipped up in the air, then landed on his feet. A split second later, he tackled Deacon Tyler again, clearly stunning the entire team. Coach Stydahar ran onto the field, screaming, "Hell, that guy can play for me anytime!"

Deacon Tyler got up and playfully slapped Richard across the helmet. "Good job, man."

"Thanks," Richard responded.

As the offense walked back toward the huddle, several of the defensive players yelled their encouragement at Richard. "I knew I had made the team then," Richard said. "They did their best, but they couldn't knock me off my feet."

Toward the end of camp, Richard was signed to the team for a total salary of $4,500. At that time, there were no signing bonuses in football. The agreement stipulated that 75% of the total salary would be paid throughout the twelve-week season, and the remaining 25% would be paid at the end of the season. If they happened to make the playoffs, each team member would make some extra cash, dependent on how far they progressed.

Once Richard made the team, it became apparent to him that the Rams' playbook was significantly more difficult to learn than anything he had studied either at Scottsbluff Junior College or in the army sports programs. "Before, I just learned simple plays with simple routes we ran. Now I had to learn 10 times the number of plays, plus audibles and all the plays and patterns the other receivers and defense were running, plus all the blocking schemes. It was a lot of work, but I had to do it."

Toward the end of practice the first week, quarterback Bob Waterfield walked up to Richard and said, "You better learn these damn plays or you won't make it here. I don't care how fast you are."

"I'm putting time in every day on the playbook," Richard replied.

"That may not be enough. See some of the veteran receivers."

The Rams had a wily veteran receiver named Tom Fears. "Fears was a well-respected player that had been through the NFL wars already. Everybody respected him. Later on, he would be in the Hall of Fame in Canton, Ohio," Richard noted. "Well, Fears had shown some interest in helping me and I took advantage of it. I constantly asked him questions about the playbook."

Late at night, when everyone was in their rooms, Richard would walk down the hallway to Fears' room, banging on the door to ask permission to enter. "Every time I banged on his door, he had some blues music playing, a song called 'Night Train' by the artist Buddy Morrow. Night after night I went to his room and every time the same song was playing. He got mad at me a few times, but he still worked with me on the offensive plays. Eventually, a few guys on the team started calling me 'Night Train.' I didn't like the nickname, but they thought it was real funny. I kept asking them to call me Dick or Richard, anything but Night Train."

During training camp, Woodley Lewis and Richard were becoming fast friends. They roomed together during camp and throughout the season during their road games.

"Woodley was a great ball player," Richard commented. "Man, could he run. He was quick, agile, and aggressive and a great friend to me during my Rams years. He had a nickname of 'Chopper,' but to tell you the truth, I'm not sure why. Maybe because he ate so much. I don't know." Richard went on to comment, "Me and Woodley weren't the biggest guys back then and we used to kid each other about gaining some weight. We ate all the time, but couldn't gain any weight. I kept telling him that he was gonna get hurt returning kickoffs."

"Why would I be the one to get hurt?" Woodley asked.

"Hell, just look at how skinny you are," Richard said.

"You're just as skinny as me!"

"Yeah, but I'm tougher," Richard retorted.

"That's a damn laugh!" Woodley countered sharply. "Next time you're on offense, just bring your skinny butt around my way, I'll show you who's too skinny!"

Richard also recalled how good Woodley could kick a football. "Lou Groza was the man back then. Groza could kick better than anyone else. I think they called him the 'toe.' But, I'll tell you what, Woodley could kick a damn ball just as good, but nobody would admit it though."

As the season started, the Rams had what appeared to be a

good solid team, with a decent chance to repeat as NFL champs. Traveling with the team was a new experience for Richard. Every opponent tried to beat them even more than usual since they were defending their title. This in itself put lots of pressure on Richard to perform at a very high level week after week. "The constant pressure was something I wasn't used to," he said. "But, with the solid group of guys around me, I quickly adapted to it."

While on the road, most of the guys on the team played cards for money. They would play in their respective rooms, or gather together in one player's room and have a gigantic game going. "Gambling was a way of life for us," Richard recalled. "It was also a good way to make some extra money, especially for a guy like me that grew up around the card game." On one particular road trip, Richard and Woodley had an excellent run of luck against their teammates and they were able to take all of their per diem money for food. "We had this big game going in our room. We took all their cash and watched them all walk out with their heads hanging like beat dogs. Woodley and I really were laughing it up."

Later that day several of their teammates came knocking on the door, literally begging for some money so they could eat lunch and supper. "We just told them no," he said. "We won it fair and square and they knew the risks going into the game. I don't know what they did for food that day, but they didn't get the loot from us."

On another road trip, the team stayed in a motel that had private kitchens in each room. Most of the players couldn't cook, so they had to go out and eat anyway. Fortunately, Richard and Woodley could cook and the rest of their team found out soon enough. "We were in Chicago to play the Bears and Woodley says to me 'Let's go eat, Train.' I said, 'Hell no! We've got a kitchen, let's use it.' I think on this particular trip we had taken some of the guys' per diem money again and feelings were running hot."

"Chopper Lewis comes back from the store with the bags of goods and I start cooking it up. It's smelling real good pretty soon and the next thing I know, there's a knock at our door. Some of our guys down the hall smelled the stuff and begged for a little." Richard continued his story, "Well, these same guys were the ones who lost their money and we just told them no. Now they had lost out both ways."

"Train, why would you treat us that way?" one player asked.

"You lost it all gambling, that ain't my fault!" Richard said.

"Yeah, but you're the one who took it from me. Just give me some of that good smelling food you got in there."

"Nope. We're gonna have that for the next two days. Besides, we didn't get enough for the whole damn team to eat," Richard replied.

The same day, at a team meeting, the coaches made some comment about Richard and Woodley being such good cooks. They also mentioned how they made up all this nice food and wouldn't share it. "Woodley and I just kept our cool. We just smiled at them and let it pass."

The next day, Richard and Woodley repeated the same act, except this time they cooked up some nice steaks. "We even opened up our door into the hallway, just so the guys would be sure to smell the aroma. Sure enough, they came down to our room again, just begging for some steak dinner. I think we just wanted to prove a point. If you're gonna gamble with professionals, you're gonna pay the price. I do recall that none of the coaches ever gambled with us. I guess the word got out about our abilities in that area."

After the season started, the game intensity increased each week. "I was real nervous that first few weeks, but looking back on it, that was the best thing that could have happened to me. It taught me a lot of respect about the players and my responsibility to the Rams team. I didn't know it at the time, but that year would be the most enjoyable of my NFL career. I was just trying to make the guys respect and trust me on the field and I didn't have time to stop and 'smell the roses' along the way. I kind of thought it would always be that way."

One of the usual perks of being on a championship team was access to the rich and famous people who followed the team. The Rams were no exception to this rule. A local Los Angeles businessman who owned a large appliance store always came to the games. "I think he was a friend of the owner," Richard said. The businessman owned several large boats at the marina, and he made them all available to the team. On Mondays, the day off after their usual Sunday games, several selected members of the team usually showed up at the marina to use the man's boats. "This guy had a 90-foot boat and a speedboat too. We'd all pile on the big yacht and cruise out into the harbor, well away from shore. Then a few of us would always jump into the speedboat, which we had towed behind the yacht, and go speeding around until the gas ran out.

"Well, one Monday, one of our players, a guy named Vitamin T. Smith, was really drunk. He demanded to get on the speedboat with us, but some of the guys were afraid he'd fall overboard and drown. We really tried to talk him out of it, but he got real mad at us, so we let him get on board. Once he got on it, he took control of it and he was really scaring us with his wild driving," Richard recalled.

"On top of that, another player, Norb Hecker, had left his wife on the yacht and he winds up on the speedboat with us. His wife tried to talk him into staying with her, but we knew Norb wanted to be around a couple of the nice looking young ladies we took with us on the speedboat. I think he just told his wife he'd be back in a minute," he continued.

"Apparently, Norb's wife had just given him a new suede jacket and she made it clear she didn't want it to get wet. Norb assured her it would be safe. Well, once we got on the speedboat, Norb starts snuggling up to one of the cute ladies and the next thing we know, she's saying she's cold and all. Norb just gives her his new suede jacket, but you got to remember, Vitamin T. is driving the boat. He's scaring the hell out of us and we're getting close to the dock, so we just make him pull the boat up and stop. The little thing wearing Norb's jacket starts to get out, but a wave hits us and she flies into the water. We're just all rolling around laughing real hard as Norb pulls her out. We look up and see his soaking wet jacket, and the expression on Norb's face is priceless."

A few of the players and their dates piled out of the speedboat and stayed on the dock. "They probably didn't want to hear Norb's wife lay into him back on the yacht," Richard said. "But I didn't want to miss it." As they returned to the yacht, they were all climbing aboard when Norb's wife walked up. Once she saw the soaking jacket and Norb's face, the sparks really started to fly. "She wanted to know how the jacket got wet and Norb didn't," Richard continued. "Finally, the truth came out and man, is she mad. Most of the guys were laughing so hard they started crying."

Once, on a Friday night before a home game on Sunday, Richard got a call from a local black entertainer/singer, Billy Eckstine. He and Billy had recently become friends. Billy was a standout singer in Los Angeles, and had invited Richard to accompany some of his friends to a performance of an up-and-coming black singer, Dinah Washington. "Dinah was becoming a legend. She was well-known across the country, even at an early age. When Dinah sang, she packed the house," Richard remarked. "I felt fortunate to be invited to one of her performances. Little did I know that many years later my friendship stemming from that night would lead to bigger things. We went to the show and everyone was totally amazed by Dinah. Man, she was something wonderful."

As the season wore on, a lot of the players on the Rams team continued to gamble both at home and on the road. "It was just a way to stay loose and a great way to make some money, if you knew what you were doing," Richard said. "We didn't bet on the games, just our private card games and maybe some craps games."

One weekend, Richard, Woodley Lewis, and a running back named Tank Younger were involved in a gambling spree in Los Angeles. "We started Friday night after practice and it continued all weekend, even after the Sunday game, which we won. Finally, Sunday night, we're at this player's house and we don't think anyone knows where we are. We hear a knock at the door and Woodley gets real nervous."

Richard continued with his story, saying, "Tank walks over to the door and peeps through the eye hole. He turns around, looking at Woodley and says, 'Man, you're in trouble, big time.' It was Woodley's wife, standing on the porch, along with his two kids and their dog. She was really mad. So mad she couldn't talk straight," he continued.

"Well, after she rang the doorbell a few more times, she starts yelling through the door at him. She says, 'Woodley, I know you're in there. I told you I don't approve of no gambling!

Since you don't care about me, I'm gonna leave the kids and dog right here on the porch.'" She then turned and walked away, leaving the kids and dog right there.

Richard continued, "Woodley ran out the door after her, but she just kept walking. I know they made up later, but the bad thing was, she blamed it all on me. Hell, I didn't force him to gamble; he wanted to do it. I guess she thought I made him stay there all weekend."

The soap opera atmosphere of that season never seemed to stop. A few weeks after that problem, Tank Younger got into some difficulty with his family. Richard recalled the circumstances. "Tank by nature was a gentle man. He was extremely tough on the football field, but in private, he was not that way. Apparently, his wife's mother comes over to his house, uninvited, and starts yelling and screaming at him for his off the field activities, like gambling. I guess Tank didn't think it was her business. One thing led to another and Tank just slapped her.

"I get this call from Tank. He's in jail and I have to go get him out. It was real bad for him. I know he hadn't been married too long and I think his new wife and mother-in-law wanted to run his life."

Life with the Rams continued to be like a soap opera. Every player had his problems, just like any person in regular life would. "You can't separate people from their personal lives just because they're professional athletes. They have just the same temptations that we all have. It just takes a strong person to overcome these problems, no matter what the circumstances."

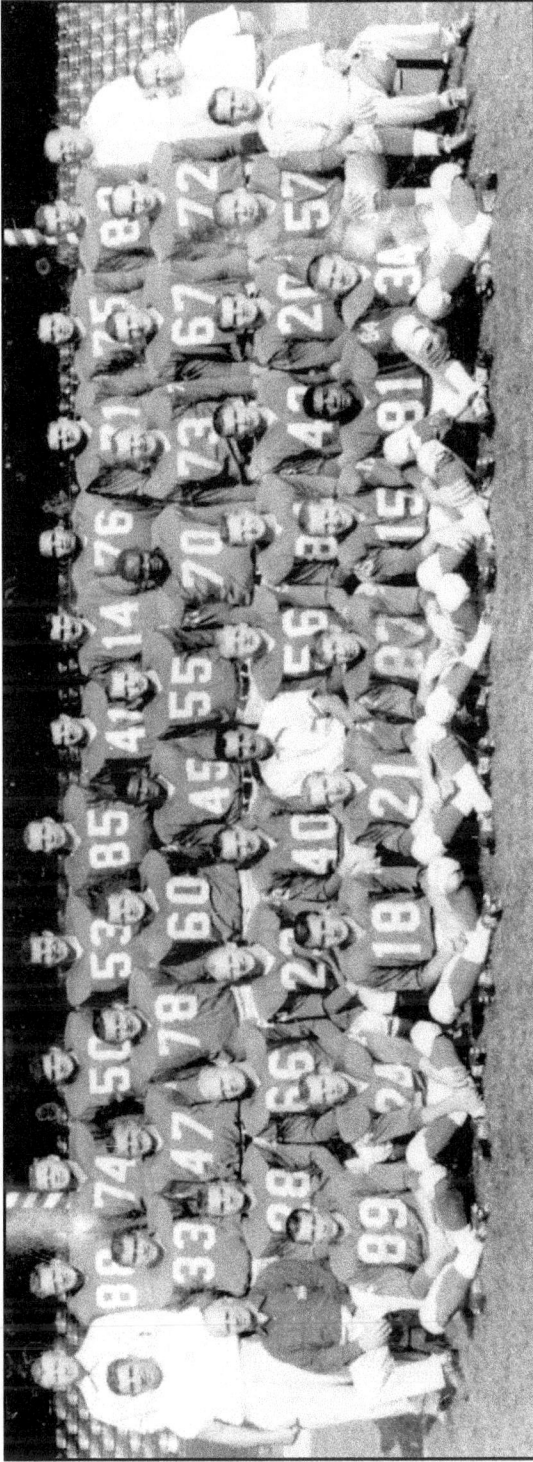

Detroit Lions, 1960. Richard Lane is #81, bottom row, second from right.

Anderson High School, Austin, Texas, 1944. Richard is #75, top row, center.

Sanford and Son poster.

Richard's Pro Football Hall of Fame Induction Ceremony, Canton, Ohio, 1974.

With Los Angeles Rams, 1952.

With Los Angeles Rams, 1952.

Richard as a Detroit Lion, 1962.

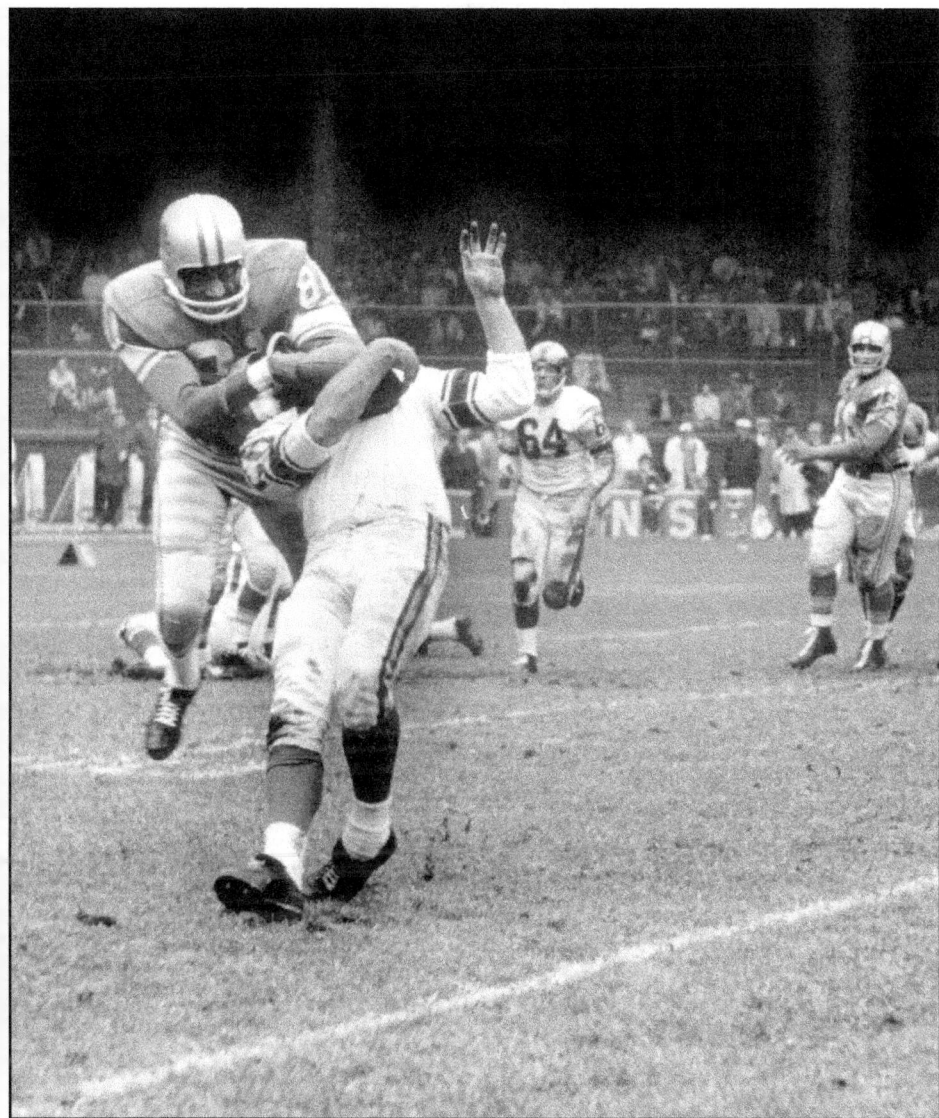

Richard tackling Los Angeles Rams receiver Jon Arnett in 1962. This play forever changed NFL rules regarding high tackling as the facemask tackle was outlawed.

STATE OF MICHIGAN

MICHIGAN SENATE

Special Tribute

MR. RICHARD "NIGHT TRAIN" LANE

WE ARE PLEASED TO OFFER THIS SPECIAL TRIBUTE OF THE VERY HIGHEST PRAISE, GRATITUDE, COMMENDATION, AND THANKSGIVING TO MR. RICHARD "NIGHT TRAIN" LANE AS HE IS INDUCTED INTO THE AFRO AMERICAN SPORTS HALL OF FAME, A MEMBER OF THE ALL-TIME, ALL-PRO TEAM IN THE NATIONAL FOOTBALL LEAGUE. MR. LANE ACCUMULATED A COMBINED TOTAL OF 68 INTERCEPTIONS, PLACING HIM SECOND ONLY TO EMLEN TUNNELL ON THE NFL'S ALL-TIME PRO LIST. HE RETIRED AFTER THIRTEEN SEASONS AND IS STILL ACCLAIMED AS PROFESSIONAL FOOTBALL'S FINEST CORNERBACK. IN 1965 HE JOINED THE FRONT OFFICE OF THE DETROIT LIONS, AND IN 1975 MAYOR COLEMAN YOUNG APPOINTED HIM DIRECTOR OF THE DETROIT POLICE ATHLETIC LEAGUE. MR. LANE HAS ALWAYS HAD A GREAT CONCERN FOR YOUNG PEOPLE AND HAS SERVED AS DIRECTOR OF THE SOUTH WEST YOUTH PROGRAM IN CHICAGO AS WELL AS OPPORTUNITY DIRECTOR FOR MAYOR CAVANAUGH'S DETROIT YOUTH PROGRAM. TRULY, HE IS A WORTHY AND VALUABLE ADDITION TO THE AFRO AMERICAN SPORTS HALL OF FAME, AND MR. LANE HAS OUR HEARTIEST CONGRATULATIONS AS HE TAKES HIS RIGHTFUL PLACE AMONG THE SPORTS GREATS OF OUR TIME.

A man's happiness and success in life will depend not so much upon what he has, or upon what position he occupies, as upon what he is, and the heart he carries into his position.
—S. J. Wilson

To be what we are, and to become what we are capable of becoming, is the only end of life.
—Robert Louis Stevenson

Ideas are, in truth, forces. Infinite, too, is the power of personality. A union of the two always makes history.
—Henry James

The secret of success is constancy to purpose.
—Benjamin Disraeli

LET IT BE KNOWN, That we take great pleasure in offering this Special Tribute of recognition, commendation, and appreciation to Mr. Richard Lane, affectionately known as "Night Train" for his powerful playing style in football. His brilliant expertise and consistent record of excellence have brought him the honour of induction into the Afro American Sports Hall of Fame. As a rookie with the Los Angeles Rams, Mr. Lane intercepted fourteen passes and in doing so set a league record. His great talents and commitment to success afforded him the opportunities to play with the St. Louis Cardinals and the Detroit Lions football teams. He accumulated a career total of sixty-eight interceptions, placing him second only to Emlen Tunnell on the National Football League's All-Time Pro list. In 1965 he retired after thirteen seasons and is still acclaimed as professional football's finest cornerback.

Although retired from active play, Mr. Lane has by no means left the sports scene. In 1965 he joined the front office of the Detroit Lions, giving freely of his experience and dedication to the team he served and loved so well as Number 81. Mayor Coleman Young acknowledged his countless contributions to the sports world by naming him director of the Detroit Police Athletic League in 1975. Mr. Lane has always had a great concern for young adults enthusiastically involving himself with myriad youth programs including service as director of the South West Youth Program in Chicago and as youth opportunity director under Mayor Cavanaugh's administration in Detroit.

IN SPECIAL TRIBUTE, Therefore, This document is signed and dedicated in recognition and appreciation of Mr. Richard "Night Train" Lane—renowned sports figure, friend and counselor to innumerable young adults, community activist, and outstanding administrator. We join with his beloved family, his many friends, and the officers and members of the Afro American Sports Hall of Fame in extending our best wishes to him for continued success and happiness as he is lauded for his invaluable contributions. It is our hope that he will accept this Special Tribute as evidence of the great respect and high esteem in which he is held by the Michigan Legislature.

I will demand a commitment to excellence and to victory, and this is what life is all about.
—Vince Lombardi

Everywhere in life, the true question is not what we gain, but what we do.
—Thomas Carlyle

Each honest calling, each walk of life, has its own elite, its own aristocracy based on excellence of performance.
—James Bryant Conant

Good men are the stars, the planets of the ages wherein they live, and illustrate the times.
—Ben Jonson

SENATOR JACKIE VAUGHN III
Associate President Pro Tempore
Third Senatorial District
The Eighty-third Legislature
At Lansing
September 13, 1986

State of Michigan tribute to Richard.

Ballantine Belles Inc.

presents

A "Memorial Tribute To Dinah"

Saturday, December 17, 1983
8:00 p.m.

Paradise Theatre (Orchestra Hall)
3711 Woodward Ave. Detroit, Michigan

*Booklet from 1983
Memorial Tribute to
Dinah Washington.*

*While Richard was working for PAL in 1977, he posed with (from left)
Richard Lane, "Spanky" in* Our Gang *series, unknown actor, "Stymie" in*
Our Gang, *and actor Forrest Tucker.*

FOR GOOD HOME COOKED FOOD...

TRY El Taco

STOP

11810 Dexter Near Tuxedo • Detroit, Michigan • TO 9-9 0
Open from 11:00 AM until 4:00 AM • Weekends until 5:00 AM

Dick "Night Train" Lane • your HOSTS • Dinah Washington Lane

FEATURING:

Mexican Tacos • Enchiladas • Tamales
Texas Steaks • Mexican Cornbread
Southern Bar-B-Que
Home Made Pies and Cakes
• We also have 'Soul Food •
'Mama' Ethel Harrison is your cook when Dinah
is 'On the Road'

Richard's El Taco Restaurant in Detroit, Michigan.

Detroit Police Athletic League photo.

The Hall of Fame class of 1974. Richard is second row from top, far left.

Richard meeting Dallas Cowboy executive Tex Schramm.

Dinah Washington

*Richard at
Detroit's Tiger Stadium.
The Lions played here
as well as the
Tigers baseball team.*

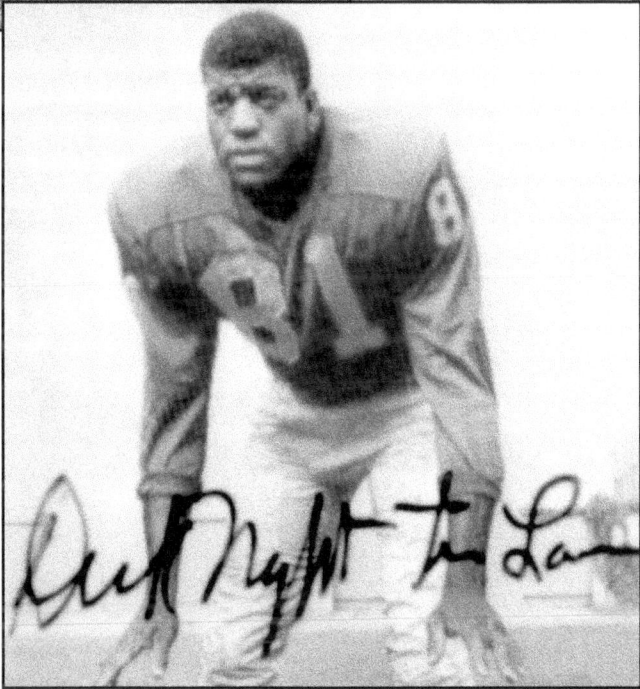

*NFL Hall of
Fame trading
card.*

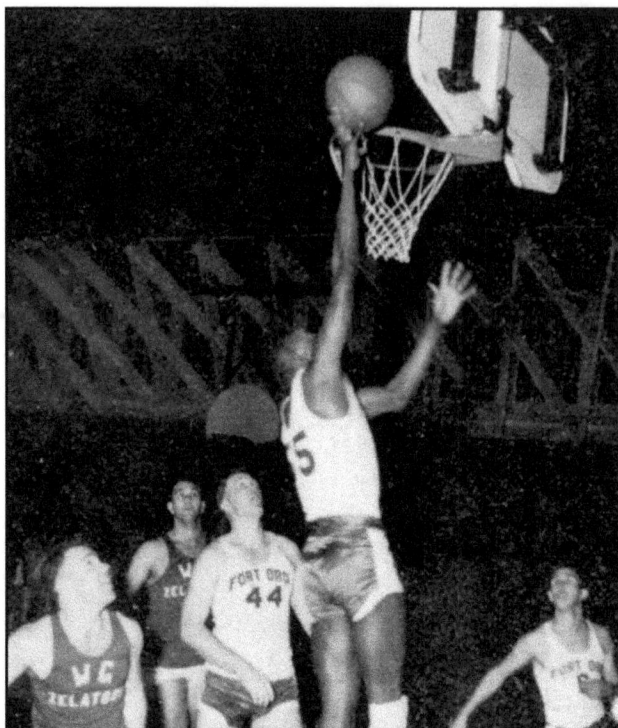

Richard going for a layup while playing for the Fort Ord Warriors.

Fort Ord Warriors.

*Richard and his Fort Ord
Warriors exiting a plane.
Richard is on the bottom row,
fifth from the left.*

*Richard
"Night Train"
Lane*

Richard, along with his son Richard, and Detroit Tigers baseball player Ron LeFlore.

Chapter Eight

SETTING NEW RECORDS

As soon as the season began in Los Angeles, Richard immediately made an impact on the team. Little did he know that his impact would set an NFL record in 1952 that still stood in 1999—a record that many football purists believe will never be broken.

During the early part of the season, the Rams played the Washington Redskins. At that time, the Redskins had a famous running back named Charlie Justice. His nickname was "Choo Choo."

"I think he got that name because he could run so fast," Richard recalled.

During the course of the game, the intensity level was rising and the hitting was ferocious on both sides of the ball. Choo Choo made an end sweep with Richard and the rest of the defense in hot pursuit. A moment later the collision took place as Richard tackled Justice with a blinding hit. After the pileup was cleared by the officials, Choo Choo laid on the ground in pain, the main recipient of Richard's strong technique. "The tackle broke his collar bone," Richard said. "It was a good clean shot."

Since Choo Choo Justice was so famous at the time, losing a player of his stature was sure to make headlines—and make headlines it did. The next day the sports page read, "Night Train derails Choo Choo."

"Until that time I hadn't liked my nickname, but that brought so much attention to me, I couldn't pass up the opportunity," he said.

That was definitely the case. In training camp, Richard had even approached Rams owner Dan Reeves to complain about the moniker, thinking the term was a derogatory remark. Luckily, it turned out the Rams owner was unable to dissuade the veteran players from calling rookies anything they wanted to. One of the Rams veterans once told Reeves that rookies don't pick their own names. So the name "Night Train" was bantered about the complex with daily regularity. "I knew then that the name would be with me forever," Richard said. From then on, the "Train" derailments happened with forceful regularity in the NFL.

As the season wore on, Richard was closing in on the single season interception record of 13 picks. At that time, the NFL season consisted of 12 games, and to average at least one grab a game was outstanding. Reporters came up to Richard after games, as he approached the record, asking him what he thought of it. "To tell you the truth, I didn't know what the record was in 1952," he said. "I was just glad to have a job with the Rams."

At the end of the 1952 season, Richard's rookie year, he assumed many people would equal or break his interception record in the coming years. "I figured that somewhere down the road, some young hotshot defender would beat my record." After some reflection, Richard continued his assessment of the still standing feat. "Now, looking back on it, I'm not so sure it will happen. Back then we always played man on man, which allowed a cornerback to be in a position to pick off lots of passes. Today's teams play lots of zone defense. You have to cover an area as opposed to man coverage. The possibility of grabbing as many errant passes isn't so great."

Throughout the remainder of the year in 1952 it became a common occurrence for a player to be hit by "The Train." His vicious tackles were a big event in any game, and being a rookie just added to the intensity of the competition. His bruising style of play served as the cornerstone for all cornerbacks in the league. Many of the great "corners" of that era, like Herb Adderley of Green Bay and Lennie Lyles of Baltimore, tried to pattern their play after him. It was a good pattern to pursue.

Several players and coaches of that era spoke in glowing terms of Night Train's abilities. They spoke of his gambling style, along with his speed and aggressiveness on the field, no matter the situation. They talked of being a cornerback in the NFL and the requirements it took to succeed. Detroit Lions coach George Wilson once remarked, "The cornerback has the toughest post on the defense. He must have the speed to cover the wideouts, the agility and strength to stop the run, and the bruising power to tackle big backs like Jim Brown and Jim Taylor."

When asked how he picked off so many passes his rookie year, Richard said, "You just have to play the percentages. You can't play a guessing game or they'll beat you most of the time. Pursuit angles are very important in football and speed is the great equalizer."

Gambling on defense was and still is a no-no in the NFL. Every player has a certain responsibility and an area to cover on the field. But Richard was the ultimate gambler. He made his gambling tendencies known by virtue of his plays. He admitted as much. "I liked to gamble. It looked like I wasn't covering my man, but in reality, I had him locked into my sights, trying to bait him and the quarterback."

Richard's defensive abilities grew so much and so quickly that the Rams even had a term for a defensive play designed for him. The play was called "44 Intercept" and it worked like this— the defense had certain assignments, but Richard was free to do what he wanted on the field. "It really freed me up to make some plays," he said. "I picked off fourteen balls, but I must have dropped at least twenty-five more I should have grabbed."

As George Wilson remarked once, "Gambling was the only way Train knew how to play football. He went for the ball more times than not and when he got it, he just killed you. In most gambling situations he won. He just played the percentages."

Many players explained their strategies of covering an offensive receiver. They talked of watching their eyes, their feet, even their helmets. But Richard had another theory he practiced to perfection. "The eyes lie and the feet deceive, so I just watched the belt buckles."

Richard seemed to always be in the "dog house" of Rams coach Hampton Pool. Things just didn't work out between them on or off the field. "I didn't like playing for Hamp," he recalled. "His theories were great and all, but he just didn't seem to care for us as players. He was real different from Coach Stydahar."

The Rams finished up the 1952 season with an overall record of 9-3. They tied for first in their division, but eventually lost to Detroit in their divisional playoff game by a score of 31-21. Richard was previously injured before that contest and he did not play in the game. "I was really disappointed I couldn't play in that game," he said. "I had set the interception record for the year and it would have been the icing on the cake to play in that divisional contest, but it just wasn't meant to be." He concluded, "My interception return average was about twenty yards a pick and I felt real sure I could contribute to the Rams in the playoffs."

The next year, 1953, the Rams finished with a record of 8-3-1 and tied for third in their division. The team didn't compete in the playoffs. Richard recalled them being a good solid team again, but as luck would have it, the bounces of the ball didn't go their way. "The second year in the league I felt much more comfortable with my cornerback position and I thought we'd make the playoffs again, but we made too many mistakes. I think I only picked off three passes that year, so I guess it couldn't be considered too good."

At the end of the 1953 campaign, Richard was upset with team management, notably the Rams owner, Dan Reeves. Richard thought he was being seriously underpaid for his on-field achievements and he made it clear to Reeves he wanted compensation for his new interception record. Reeves didn't make any overtures toward Richard which would make him feel like a valued team member, so Richard asked to be traded, hopefully to the Chicago Cardinals, who had just hired Rams head coach Joe Stydahar after the season was over. In a short time Reeves gave Richard his request, and the trade was complete.

Chapter Nine

On to Chicago

The Chicago Cardinals can lay claim to the distinction of being the oldest continuously run professional football team in the country. The team, founded in 1898, has had many names dating back to their inception: Chicago Cardinals, Racine Cardinals, The Normals, Morgan Athletic Club, St. Louis Cardinals, Phoenix Cardinals, and most recently, the Arizona Cardinals.

Nobody was happier to see Night Train Lane in Chicago than the Cardinals owner, Walter Wolfner. The Cardinals had been suffering through dismal records the last few years, and the addition of Lane was a monumental move for the team. Several sports magazines noted that the trade with the Los Angeles Rams, which sent Lane and tackle Len Teeuws to Chicago in return for Cardinal players Don Paul and Volney Peters, could be considered the best trade in team history.

When the plane landed in Chicago in the late summer of 1954, Richard was greeted at the airport by Walter Wolfner, owner of the team. As Richard and Wolfner shook hands, Wolfner handed him a $1,000 bill. To say Richard was astonished was a big understatement. "I had never seen a $1,000 bill before. And really, I probably didn't think they even existed."

Wolfner got right to the point by saying, "Night Train, welcome to Chicago."

"Thanks, Mr. Wolfner," Richard replied.

"This money is just the first level of appreciation we're extending to you."

Richard just stared at the bill, completely flabbergasted, before finally saying, "Man, I've never seen one of these."

"Get used to it. There's more where that came from," Wolfner strongly replied.

"Yes, sir!" Richard shot back with a firm voice.

That first year Richard made the timely sum of $7,000 for the 1954 season. "It was a nice raise from the Rams money, and I thought it was just the tip of the iceberg. But not only did the money dry up quickly, I came to see that the team was badly disorganized with only a few of the players having the proper mental attitude to win." Richard concluded, "I had no idea the next six years would be the most unjoyful of my entire fourteen-year career."

As Richard and Geraldine settled into life in the Windy City, things were looking very positive for them. "I was glad to be out of Los Angeles and that situation. I had felt entirely under-appreciated in L. A., and hoped the new surrounding in Chicago would lend itself to a stronger marriage between myself and Geraldine."

As Geraldine looked for work in town, Richard started meeting all his new teammates at the Cardinals complex on the city's south side. The Chicago Bears were an NFL powerhouse even in the early years, and the fact that the Cardinals shared the same city with them only added fuel to the football fire. Back then, even a losing season by one team could be considered somewhat salvageable by beating the cross-town rival.

The 1954 Cardinal team finished with a poor record of 2-10, which placed them sixth in their division. "I really didn't see the train wreck of a season coming until it was too late," Richard said. "But even if I had seen it happening, I couldn't have done anything about it. We weren't even halfway close to being a playoff team. Even powerhouse coach Joe Stydahar couldn't get us going straight." Indeed, the only good thing Richard recalled about his first year in Chicago, was that he led the league for a second time in interceptions, with a yearly total of 10.

The next year, 1955, the team finished up with a record of 4-7-1, which tied them for fourth in their division. It was a dismal failure by most any football standards. "I tried to get the guys playing harder by using my past experiences with the Rams. But I couldn't get the point across. It just seemed like they weren't dedicated to trying to win."

During the 1955 season, it became clear that the $1,000 bill Wolfner gave Richard was nothing more than a smoke screen. The fiscal spending by Wolfner was becoming a joke within the team ranks. They traveled by train and bus whereas the other NFL teams usually traveled by chartered airplane. Some of the shorter journeys they took were understandable, but the cross-country trips were made even more difficult by their mode of travel.

"I recall a few times we traveled by train to play some tough games out of town. By the time we got there we actually felt worse than before we left. The train ride was just horrible." Richard talked to Stydahar about it, but the coach had no answer.

"Train, I don't control the travel arrangements," Stydahar said.

"Coach, some of the guys wanted me to talk to you, since I had some seniority, and you and I go back a few years," Richard said.

"I understand, believe me. But Wolfner handles all this. I've talked to him about it, but I don't think it's ever going to change."

"Coach, that's part of the reason we can't win. Our attitude is bad and it starts from the top on down. They see everything being penny pinched and they don't understand."

"Train, it's always about the money, the bottom line. I can't control that," Stydahar remarked. "We've just got to play our best."

Richard reflected back on the team and thought Wolfner may have stepped in above his head when he took over. A salary cap restriction didn't exist back then, and the richest owners just tried to buy the best players. There were no TV deals to be made, and therefore the money disparity between the teams was evident in every respect.

The only good moment Richard recalled about the 1955 season was an NFL record he set for a pass reception, which was later broken by another player on another team. He caught a pass from quarterback Ogden Compton in a game against Green Bay. He never stopped until he reached the goal line, 98 yards away. Richard was playing offense, defense, and some special teams also. "Playing three ways was extremely difficult. You just never seemed to leave the field. I remember many times after some of those games I was so tired, I literally couldn't think straight. So, me catching that pass for 98 yards like that was very satisfying to me. It for sure was one of the highlights of my career."

On top of all the team troubles, Geraldine was continually drinking again, sometimes not even making any attempt to hide it. "Looking back on it, it was very clear she couldn't beat the addiction," Richard said. "The change of scenery to Chicago was a total failure in many respects both personally and professionally."

Richard again tried to get her counseling for her alcoholism, but during those days fighting the uphill battle with either drugs or alcohol was usually a lost cause. The treatment centers were not as well trained in helping people with addictions as they are today, and most attempts at rehab were met with total failure.

Geraldine would not be home at night when Richard came in after practice, and he had to make the rounds of the local night club scene to find her, either with her cronies or many times completely alone. The times she was at home, Richard could smell the booze on her breath and he always confronted her with it, but to no avail. "It was tearing at me all the time," he said. "I loved Geraldine a lot. But the booze was her main companion. It had started back in the army days when we were married, and had continually gotten worse. I don't know if alcoholism is hereditary or not, but I found out later her father was a drunk too. I really think we would have stayed married forever if it hadn't been for that. I just really hated her drinking so much."

Since Richard had made a name for himself in the Rams organization with his record-setting fourteen interceptions in 1952, things on the football field weren't any easier either. The players on all the opposing teams were out to get him, to prove a point.

Dirty play was evident in several ways back in the early days and all the players paid the price for lax enforcement of the rules. Injuries were a weekly reminder of their rough playing style.

Richard recalled many instances where he would be running down the field and an opposing player would just "cold cock him" across the face or nose. "I'd just be running downfield and the next thing I know, I'm getting a fist or forearm across the face."

But the retaliation in the NFL was usually swift and deadly. Players on the receiving end of such actions just bided their time during the game and struck when the opportunity presented itself. "If me or one of my guys got hit with a cheap shot, the time would always come where we could get even. Usually, the refs didn't call it for some reason or another, so whenever there was a big pileup of players, we always got even with some cheap shots of our own."

Richard recollected a particular incident. "One time, Ollie Matson was constantly being grabbed by his facemask. He begged and pleaded with the refs to stop it, but his pleas were falling on deaf ears. I saw him walk up to one ref right after a play and calmly say to him, 'Ref, you gotta listen to me. You gotta keep those damn guys from grabbing my mask.'"

"Matson, just you keep playing and let us handle the calls," he responded.

"But, ref, you're not making the calls!"

The ref just stared him down and eventually Matson walked off toward his huddle. A few plays later, the same guy grabbed Matson's mask. This time Matson took care of it himself. "I saw him just rip the guy's helmet off and push his head down into the mud. He was rubbing it real hard. He then beat on the guy's head for a second. As a fight was about to break out, Ollie looked up at the ref and said, 'You didn't want to handle it, so I did!'"

It wasn't like the Cardinals didn't have some great players on the team. Future Hall of Famer Matson, a 6-foot-2 inch, 210-pound halfback, was already with the team when Richard showed up. Matson had been a spectacular player in college and his athletic ability continued to shine in the pro ranks. "Ollie was one of the best and toughest players I ever saw," Richard said. "He was extremely durable and dependable."

Matson's All-American status in college led him to make the U.S. track team in 1952 that went to the Olympics. Many people didn't think Matson would make the Olympic track team, but his determination and ability proved them wrong.

Richard recalled Matson being the best running back in pro football during his tenure with the Cardinals. "Nobody could outrun him at his position," he commented. "During the 1956 season, in which we finished 7-5, Ollie tied a Cardinals record for a kickoff return, running one back 105 yards," Richard said. "I think that year was his best as our running back. He got almost 1,000 yards rushing, but he had almost 400 yards in rushing called back due to penalties. It was really amazing to me."

The biggest problem with the Cardinals, as evidenced by some of their losses, was their offensive and defensive lines. The majority of football games are won or lost on the line of scrimmage. If one team can dominate the line, they can control almost every snap of the ball.

Richard told Matson that he better talk to Wolfner to get them some better linemen or they wouldn't last too long at their current rate. Matson got mad at him and said, "Hell, I can run through anyone!"

"I know you're a great runner, Ollie, but nobody can run forever. We need some bigger holes to run through."

Matson would argue with Richard about the line blocking and Richard thought Matson was just making a good show of it, just to make a point that he was tougher than anyone else. But Richard knew he was right and he figured Matson knew it as well, deep down inside.

After one very rough game, Matson was lying on the trainer's table getting his bruised body worked on. Richard walked up and looked at him, kind of staring. Matson looked up and said, "Train, just what the hell are you doing?"

"I'm looking at a man that's gonna get killed."

"To hell you say!"

"I told you to talk to them," Richard replied. "We need some better linemen. You're a damn good runner, but no one can run without some blocking."

Matson just stretched out on the table without saying another word. His refusal to argue with Richard anymore was his silent agreement to the situation. Unfortunately, for the entire team, the problem was never corrected.

As time passed in Chicago, Richard knew his rocky marriage to Geraldine was weak at best. He continually made every effort to keep her happy. He also borrowed money to buy three different restaurants over the six years they lived there. "I got to know some solid investors who wanted to put in the dough, if I'd lend my name to the businesses." He continued, "I was putting my heart and soul into football, but we weren't going anywhere, so I figured the food business might work. Little did I know, the food business was just as tough as the football world."

Richard also assumed that a new atmosphere surrounding his family might help with Geraldine's mental outlook, especially if it brought in lots of money. "I was wrong on both accounts," he said. "The restaurant I owned, El Taco Stop, ate up all my money and my investor's money too. It was too hard for me to do my thing during the day and then show up at night to oversee the businesses. I think this added burden was just another excuse for my wife to keep drinking."

As usual, gambling was a very large enterprise in Chicago, and Richard made every use of it that he could. He set up street craps games outside his restaurants and exclusive card games inside. From each enterprise, he took a healthy cut. The boxing game produced some good paydays for him as well, but so much of boxing was fixed by the promoters in that era it was tough to do it on a weekly basis.

Richard didn't particularly like the gambling business, but it could be lucrative at times. Since football didn't pay all the bills, it was almost impossible to pass up the chance. "When my creditors came calling due to my failing business, I had to try anything to make ends meet. I guess I always could have gotten a night job, but I wasn't inclined to. Here I was an All-Pro and I was struggling to make ends meet. It was a lot of hard work with very little rewards."

The remainder of Richard's time with the Cardinals never produced a true winner. The 1957 team finished 3-9, the 1958 team finished 2-9-1, and the final year of his tenure, 1959, produced a record of 2-10. The only two salvations of his time in Chicago were his teammates, a few of which became Pro Bowl players, and the fact that he was named to the Pro Bowl in 1955, 1956, and 1959.

Richard recalled a few of his prominent teammates in Chicago. "I played with Ollie Matson, Mal Hammack, Dick Nolan, Charlie Jackson, Pat Summerall, and Lindon Crow, to mention a few. It was really unfortunate we couldn't field a winning team with the talent we had. I always regretted that."

To make matters worse, Richard and Geraldine divorced in 1959. Their stormy marriage had lasted eleven years. Eleven years of intense personal problems like excessive drinking and several miscarriages. And, the last six of which constituted the roughest times in Richard's life in the NFL. "It was just awful," he said. "Six years of losing games and watching my marriage fail right before my eyes. Plus, my three businesses also were eventually lost. The only positives about my time there was the three years I spent working in the Mayor's Youth Foundation in the off-season and I became reacquainted with Dinah Washington after my divorce. Dinah and I had become good friends over the years and my wife and I had attended many of her shows. Dinah now lived in Chicago and my recent divorce opened the door for our courtship. I didn't know at the time, but we would marry four years later."

Probably the only reason Richard didn't quit the team was his fear of failure and the possibility of living a life of poverty. "So many times I wanted to quit the Cardinals, but each time I considered it, I thought about all those times in Austin when I had to work my butt off just to eat. I remember helping a guy I knew unload sweet potatoes off his truck every week. I wouldn't get paid money, he'd just give me a few potatoes to take home to Mama Ella. I always remembered traveling with the Omaha Rockets and not eating some days or at least only eating once a day. That fear put the motivation in me to succeed. It just made me work that much harder."

Richard's last year in Chicago was the 1959 season. Immediately after the season, he was traded to the Detroit Lions. The trade at that time seemed just like any other football trade to Richard, but in the end, it would prove to be a benefit to his career.

Chapter Ten

Life in Detroit

Richard's trade to the Detroit Lions was the brainchild of Detroit coach George Wilson, who wanted to build up the sagging defense of the Lions' secondary. Wilson said Richard was a gambler, but a gambler who took calculated chances. Many people in football circles thought the trade for Night Train Lane was a mistake by the Lions, but eventually it proved to be a solid move.

Over the six years Richard was in Detroit, he played in three Pro Bowls: 1961, 1962, and 1963. And the Lions were a playoff team while Richard was with them. Coach Wilson was quoted as saying, "I knew when I got Night Train that he was a winner and a gambler. I liked it that way. Sometimes he lost a gamble, but usually he won. I really wanted players who won the majority of the time."

As almost any football purist will tell you, playing the cornerback position is the most physically demanding on the field. Richard was the ultimate cornerback, and the Lions benefited from his expertise in this area. When asked about his overall playing time with the Lions, Richard remarked, "I played hard for that team. I was at the end of my career, and I think everyone, including myself, knew it. I wanted to go out big. The crowds in Detroit wanted me to make the big plays all the time and sometimes you can't."

Lions receiver Jim Gibbons once remarked, "Train's the best corner in the league. If he makes a mistake, he usually can recover. That's what separates him from the rest. His natural reflexes."

Richard was constantly bombarded with questions about his tendency to tackle the ball carrier around the head or shoulders—a technique known as the "Night Train Necktie." He commented, "My objective is to stop the ball carrier before he gains another inch. I'm usually working against receivers that try to fall forward after they're hit. So, I didn't want to hit them in the legs. There's nothing I hated worse than a damn first down! It usually meant I had to stay out there longer. If I hit them around the neck, lots of times it's over then and there."

The man who played opposite Richard's left cornerback position was right corner Dick LeBeau. LeBeau was the exact opposite of his playing partner. He very rarely gambled on defense. Instead of taking a chance on an interception as a gambler would, he was very content to let his man catch a short pass in front of him, just to make sure the long ball didn't beat him. These two men together comprised a strong Lions backfield.

In the 1960 season, Detroit finished with a record of 7-5, which tied them for second in their division. This was a huge step for Richard since leaving the Chicago Cardinals, whose last campaign in 1959 was 2-10. "It was great to be playing winning football again," Richard said.

One of the most famous moments of Richard's career, of which there were many, was a game in 1960, played against the powerful Baltimore Colts and their famous quarterback, future Hall of Fame player Johnny Unitas. As the clock ran down, the Lions held a slim 23-17 lead. Unitas was marching the Colts methodically downfield for a score, which would have given the Lions a fourth straight defeat very early in the season.

With the game on the line and possibly the season in the balance, Richard made what many consider the play of the season, an interception of a Unitas pass. "I picked it off at our own 20 yard line and ran it back the full 80 yards for the game winning score. I was proud of that pick since Johnny U. was the hardest to read of all the signal callers. He would constantly pump fake you, to mess you up."

Indeed, the final score of 30-17 would prove to be the season turning point for his team, who finished up 7-5. "I realized later that the interception off Unitas kind of got us going that year. I didn't realize it then, but I did later on. A fourth straight loss would have killed us."

Richard recalled making a speech at halftime of that famous game. "I remember hearing that some or all of the coaches might get fired if we kept losing and that wouldn't be fair to them. I recall making the speech, but I don't remember any of the exact words really. I was just real mad. I said something like we should be ashamed of ourselves for playing so damn bad. I guess the speech didn't hurt."

Some of his teammates recalled Richard being labeled a malcontent when he was at the Cardinals and then again upon his arrival at the Detroit Lions. Richard labeled himself differently. "I was a hard working athlete that was just tired of losing. Losing seemed to follow me everywhere. I even lost all my money in my Chicago restaurants. I first thought the players in Detroit didn't want to win bad enough and I didn't keep those feelings to myself either."

Richard finished up the story by noting, "The next week we lost at Los Angeles anyway. If we had lost to the Colts, then the Rams, we would have been 0-5 and I don't think we could have turned it around. Instead, we pulled together as a team."

The record reflects that the 1960 Lions next went to Kezar Stadium to play the San Francisco 49ers. Detroit won 24-0. "We held them to zero points," Richard proudly said. "I think that was the first time that had happened to them at home."

After the San Francisco game, the Lions went on to win five of the next six games, whereupon they earned a trip to Miami to represent the Western Division of the NFL. "We went to Miami to play in the first Playoff Bowl game, which pitted second-seeded teams against each other. I was proud of our team at that point. We started out as losers, but finished up strong."

In Miami, on January 7, 1961, the Lions won the playoff game. Playing against the Cleveland Browns, Richard rushed the kicker and blocked a PAT (Point after Touchdown). If Cleveland had made the kick, the game would have been tied, 17-17. Detroit went on to win the game by a score of 17-16. "We finished up the season winning eight times in the last ten games," he boasted. "I was really happy with our performance. I was 33 years old and still playing my favorite sport."

Indeed, the 1960 Detroit team carried lots of players who made All Pro for many years, and some who eventually made it into the Hall of Fame in Canton. The team had men on it like Glenn Davis, Jim Ninowski, Yale Lary, Harley Sewell, Howard Cassady, Wayne Walker, Grady Alderman, Joe Schmidt, Earl Morrall, Roger Brown, and Alex Karras. One of their assistant coaches was Don Shula, who 30 years later would be the winningest football coach in NFL history.

Life in Detroit continued to look up for Richard. He met a new girlfriend, Mary Cowser. They dated for a brief time and eventually married. "Mary and I hit it off immediately, but life throws you many obstacles. We ran into trouble that we couldn't straighten out. I've never really discussed our problems or the breakup of our marriage."

Although the marriage didn't last, it produced a son, Richard Lane II, who is still close to his father. "Richard is a good son to me and he gave me a wonderful granddaughter too. He and I stay in contact frequently, but since he lives in St. Louis, Missouri, it's hard to see each other a lot. We stay in contact by e-mail, letters, and the phone. A few times a year he comes to Austin to see me."

Many people have said that the first four years in Detroit marked the high point in Richard's career, and they're probably right. Even though he intercepted 14 passes in 1952, a record which still stands (in 1999), he was named to the All NFL team only once, in 1956. While in the Motor City he was named to the All League team four straight years, from 1960 to 1963.

Someone once asked Richard which cornerback resembled him the most in his style of play. "I think Lem Barney of Detroit was the closest thing to me," he said. "Jake Scott of the Dolphins was also a lot like me, but he played the safety position. Both were guys who went after the ball." He finished up by saying, "You've got to remember, playing corner, it was entirely different. You had to make the receiver run a certain way, hopefully a way he didn't want to run. If a guy was going to run a post pattern, I tried to make him run it right through me."

The 1961 season for the Lions was another winning season in which they finished up 8-5-1 and again tied for second in their division. The 1961 campaign was a big year for Richard in two ways—two ways he will always be remembered for in football history. "I guess I'll take some history with my name on it any way I can get it," he commented. "But I really wasn't too proud of one of them."

The most notorious day that Richard affected pro football was later referred to as "The Day Face Mask Tackling Was Outlawed." It is very difficult indeed for one man to do something in his sport that constitutes a rule change on the field. The longer, more established the sport, the harder it is to bring about a rules change. Such was the atmosphere in late 1961.

One Sunday, the Lions were playing the Rams in the L.A. Coliseum. Jon Arnett, a Rams receiver, was running down the sideline after making a catch. He had put some distance between himself and the Lions defense, everybody except Night Train Lane. Night Train was running a full sprint trying to catch Arnett before he crossed the goal line. When he leaped at Arnett, his arms were outstretched, just hoping to grab anything but air. Sure enough, he missed air, but his hand grabbed Arnett fully by the facemask. "I hit him pretty hard," Richard said firmly. "The next thing I knew, he was stretched out on the ground, not moving too much."

Most spectators that day recalled it being a very violent tackle. One which might have killed Arnett, if not for his superb physical condition. Richard recalled it differently. "I had hit lots of guys harder than that. It was just the combination of his speed and the angle I took to him."

The Rams trainers rushed over to Arnett, who lay motionless for quite a long time. Finally, the doctor gave him a dose of smelling salts and he slowly snapped out of it. Indeed, Arnett's conditioning kept him from being hurt too badly, and eventually he returned to the game.

Richard recalled the fans booing loudly at him. "I felt like they wanted to kill me. Sure, it was a big hit, but it's a big game with big guys. I wasn't intentionally trying to hurt him."

But the league saw it differently. In the off-season, the NFL ruled that no one could tackle any player by the facemask, intentional or otherwise. The league enacted stiff penalties for such actions, plus fines and game suspensions. So, Richard "Night Train" Lane became famous again. The first time setting the single season interception record, and now the no-facemask tackling rule.

The second most important part of the 1961 campaign came at season's end, in the Pro Bowl, which was played in Los Angeles in January 1962. The Pro Bowl, always played after the season is over, is meant to observe and illuminate the year's most spectacular players in a game full of such players. To be named to the Pro Bowl is about the highest honor a player can receive. Richard would eventually play in a total of six such games, but this one was special.

On Friday, two days before the game, Richard started feeling ill. He couldn't keep anything in his stomach. After consulting with a doctor, Richard was quite sure he had an appendix problem. It was a serious problem that would require surgery. But he for sure didn't want to miss the Pro Bowl at the Coliseum, the place he started his career. "I called the doctor and told him to give me some medicine, just for the pain. Anything to get me through the game."

Saturday night was by far the worst. "I felt just horrible. Couldn't sleep all night. It seemed like daybreak would never come." He continued, "If it hadn't been for the game on Sunday I would have bagged it in for sure."

Sunday morning the doctor gave Richard some pain pills, which enabled him to play without too much pain. "It let me be able to tackle the guys without passing out from the pain," he noted. "But, the whole time, I just felt weak as a kitten. I don't ever recall feeling that bad for that long." The weakness was probably brought on by lack of food for 48 hours.

Overcoming all of the appendicitis problems was tough under any circumstances, but Richard made the best of it beyond just being on the field. He scored the first touchdown for the West team with an interception, which resulted in a 42 yard run back. He played the rest of the game in an outstanding manner, which culminated in his team winning by a score of 31-30. "That game still sticks with me," he said. "I for sure played in more important games, but that game really proved I was mentally tough."

The next morning, Monday, Richard entered St. Joseph Hospital in Burbank, California, and had his appendix removed. "Man, I never thought I'd be so happy to be in a hospital bed," he said. "The food was terrible, but any food was better than what I had been through. It was wonderful just to be pain free and able to eat anything."

As time progressed in Detroit, Richard's contacts with blues singer Dinah Washington also picked up steam. Richard had parted ways with Mary Cowser for good, and his thoughts continually drifted back to Dinah. "It was very hard not to think about her. She was more famous than ever," he said. "I felt fortunate to be able to call her, much less date her. We had known each other for many years, but the timing just wasn't right. A gal like that could easily draw a long line of suitors."

Indeed, Dinah Washington was compared to Elizabeth Taylor in overall popularity. Her records didn't usually cut across cultural lines, but her songs were wonderful and enjoyed by one and all. Anyone who heard her perform could quickly reason why she was called "Queen of the Blues."

"Her voice was pure silk," he said. "I used to keep her records playing anytime I was in a room alone. I really loved her record 'Only a Moment Ago.' It really made me feel good. Sometimes guys on the team would walk into my room and her records would be playing so loud I couldn't hear them."

The relationship between Dinah and Richard was a good one. She was the most famous black female singer in America and Richard was the most famous cornerback in the NFL. It was a perfect fit in many ways. "We got along great," he added. "Our personalities were great for each other and I think we complimented each other too."

The 1962 Lions finished up with an impressive 11-3 record, which tied them for second in their division. Richard was also named to the Pro Bowl again in January 1963. But the crowning achievement of 1963 had to be the marriage of Richard and Dinah. "I was literally on top of the world," he said proudly. "I loved her a lot, and our marriage solidified our relationship."

The marriage, which was covered in *Time* magazine, also caught the media's attention in another way. Wilt Chamberlain, the famous NBA basketball player, was Richard's best man. "I had met Wilt through my sports activities and we hit if off pretty quick. Wilt was a great guy, and his presence at our wedding meant a lot to me."

Life sped up a lot for the newlywed couple. Richard had culminated the prior season with his Pro Bowl appearance and now he was on the road again, supporting his new wife. Her concerts were set up in many towns across many states. Her entourage was large, requiring Richard to share her with aher fans and the media. "I didn't care. It was just great to see her perform weekly. To know I was a part of her life in show business meant a lot to me."

Dinah had been crowned "Queen of the Blues," but Richard was quick to point out that she was more than that in many respects. "She was the queen of the blues, pop, and rhythm. We could be walking down the street and someone would yell 'Queen.' All heads would turn to see her."

On top of all of Dinah's singing abilities was the fact that she was extremely generous to any and all around her. She regularly gave back to show business just as much as she took from it. Richard recalled it this way: "She would bring lesser known talents under her wing and demand that promoters include them on her shows. Sometimes the promoters would refuse to do it and Dinah would say 'Well, then. I guess I won't be coming either.' That usually got the ball rolling again."

Sometimes in these situations, Dinah would even pay the new talent out of her own pocket. "Lots of people didn't know that," Richard said. "We got into arguments over it a few times. I'd say, what you doing that for?"

"Because they deserve a break just like me," Dinah answered back.

"Well, you can't feed everybody in town!" Richard exclaimed.

"Maybe not, but I can make sure the good black singers get a fair chance."

Dinah made such an effort of giving of herself, and her money, that she was never able to accumulate much on her own. Even after years of lucrative singing engagements she was constantly in debt. "Here I was, always having money problems with my limited football salary, losing money in restaurants and such and now Dinah was having problems too."

Dinah also took a big chance by opening her own booking agency, at a time when it was very risky for a black woman to do so. The black talent in the 1950s and 1960s usually operated within a tight culture where promoters carried a "big stick." It was one thing to be a singer and another to be a promoter or booking agent. Normally, they never crossed paths in one name. But Dinah wanted to change that stereotype.

Richard recalled Dinah's early life in Chicago. "Most people didn't know she got her start singing with the Lionel Hampton band. Hampton was a gigantic presence back then, and to be included with his performers was a big step for a singer." He continued, "Dinah was just nineteen when she started with Hampton. After she started to be recognized, she left the band and went out on her own. Then, the sky was the limit. She always had two or three hits a year on the charts."

Although Dinah had hit after hit on the black charts, she never really reached the white record buyers until 1959. That year she recorded a song called "What a Difference a Day Makes." It was an instant hit and the record solidified her both in the black and white recording community.

Richard also noted a darker side to Dinah, a side that was well known but not discussed too much. "She had been married many times. I think probably six or seven before me. I know she once said, 'I try to change men before they have a chance to change me.' Dinah was also known to be pretty rowdy at nightclubs, throwing glasses at people who interrupted her and sometimes even cussing a blue streak, but that was Dinah. I loved her just the way she was."

In 1963 the Detroit Lions finished with a record of 5-8-1, which was a huge disappointment to Richard, since the previous year they were 11-3. But the disappointments were just beginning. Richard recalled the circumstances of a late night in December 1963. "I woke up early in the morning, before the sun was up. I heard the TV blaring real loud at the end of the bed. Dinah lots of times left the TV on when she was the last one to go to sleep. I looked over and didn't see her beside me. I knew something was wrong."

Richard continued by saying, "I jumped up and found her on the floor, unconscious, but still breathing. I couldn't wake her. I called the ambulance and they took her to the hospital, but she died later that day."

It was well known that Dinah took large doses of pills to control her weight and a sleeping disorder. That, plus her frequent drinking bouts, led to an untimely demise. Richard was heartbroken in her loss. "Here we had been married less than a year and now she was dead. The whole world crashed around me."

Many people later speculated that her new marriage to Richard, the upcoming Christmas season, the opening of her new night club, the Belles, and another pill-induced diet all came together to put extreme pressure on her at one time. Richard wasn't so sure. "She had pressure her whole life. I don't think the pressure did it. She was young, 39, and everything was looking up for us. It was just bad luck. The pills and her drinking probably were the main culprits."

The funeral for Dinah was held in two cities, Chicago and Detroit, to enable her fans to see her for one last time in each place. Her husband, the famous athlete, Richard Lane, in many other circles would have drawn the majority of attention. But Richard paled in comparison to Dinah's celebrity status. "Sure I was famous in my own way, but nothing compared to her," he said. That day, though the weather was bitterly cold and snowy, it didn't deter her fans. "The two funerals drew about 30,000 people. Not too many people could draw a crowd like that, and for sure not me," he concluded.

The Chicago funeral was held in St. Luke's Baptist Church. "The church was packed full of mourners," Richard recalled. "I was on the front pew, closest to the casket. The reverend talked about Dinah and her previous time she spent at the church, when she sang in the St. Luke's gospel choir. Then, another singer, a friend of my wife, Mahalia Jackson, sang a real spiritual song to us." Afterwards, the hundreds of mourners outside the church were allowed inside to see Dinah one more time.

In all of Richard's 14-year NFL career, he had never voluntarily missed a game. However, the Sunday following his wife's death, the Lions were slated to play the Chicago Bears and

Richard wasn't there. His coach, George Wilson, knew it was best he didn't even make the effort. Lots of people thought the outcome would have been different if Richard had played, but we'll never know for sure.

After Dinah's untimely death, financial problems enveloped Richard. "Lots of her creditors came after me, thinking I had her money. Truth was, there was no money. She made over $100,000 per year the last several years of her life, but she gave most of it away. Nobody really believed me. After a while, the creditors finally stopped harassing me. It was just another bad turn in an extremely bad year."

Richard's final two years as a player in Detroit, 1964 and 1965, produced only one winning season. In 1964 they finished up 7-5-2. The 1965 campaign ended with a 6-7-1 record. He recalled the final two years solemnly, saying, "We played our best those two years, but we couldn't field a solid team. We had lots of bad breaks on the field." Not only did the team have bad breaks on the field, but Richard suffered a severe injury to his left knee early in the season, which resulted in him missing a majority of the year. "I got hurt pretty bad and never fully recovered from it. After that, I picked off only one pass that year. Finally, I had to have knee surgery. My speed just wasn't the same."

Whatever the Lions record was in any given year, the Thanksgiving Day game always marked a special occasion to the team and the fans. "No matter how poorly we were playing, on Thanksgiving Day we played our hearts out for the fans. Even if we knew the game was meaningless to our season, we put out our best effort.

"I remember my first year with the Rams. I saw the Lions play on Thanksgiving and I thought, oh man, hope I don't ever have to play on turkey day in that cold weather. Little did I know, years later, it would happen. And, years later, it turned out to be a privilege."

Chapter Eleven

Life After Football

Richard knew the decline in his football ability and his lack of playing time the prior year would not bode well for the future. Life in the big leagues is a cold hard numbers game, and every player is aware of the consequences. "Basically, you're only as good as your last game. And taken in a bigger view, you're only as good as your last year." Richard added, "When you factor in a major knee injury which made me slower, and my age, well, I knew the end was near. I just didn't want to admit it to myself or anyone else."

When training camp opened for the Lions' 1966 season, Richard was still on the team. But, during an exhibition game against the New York Giants, Richard's old teammate, Earl Morrall, threw four straight passes into Lane's zone. The last pass was for a 10 yard touchdown. Richard recalled the circumstances, "I was playing my best, but the guy just beat me for the TD. Two years before, and it wouldn't have happened."

A few days later, head coach Harry Gilmer gave Richard his release from the team. A release from the team meant he was free to pursue any team in the league for a slot on their roster. In reality, he was a "free agent" in an era when pro football really didn't have a free agency clause.

The release didn't catch Richard off guard. "I saw it coming for sure. I was 37 years old, but to tell you the truth, I still thought I could play. Like most guys in my position, I still had the fire burning in me." Indeed, he had made it through the grit, grime, and hard work of pre-season training camp, but it just wasn't meant to be. "I wouldn't have worked that hard if I didn't think my skills were good enough."

When the release came, there was no bitterness directed toward the club. He noted, "It's just part of the business. It's usually not personal. When a new coach takes over a club, that's usually the way things happen. He wants to put his stamp on the team." He concluded by saying, "You've got to remember, when I came here in 1960 they said I was washed up then. I think I made it pretty far considering I made All-Pro for three straight years, from 1961 to 1963."

Richard's place on the defensive side of the ball was taken by Bobby Thompson, a second-year player in the league. "Young players always were trying to take a veteran's slot," he said. "It's just a sign of the times. Hell, when I was young, I did the same thing. The funny thing was I still physically looked the same. I hadn't gained or lost any undue weight, but my speed had diminished."

Leaving the team the same year were standout players Yale Lary and Gary Lowe. Lary retired from the NFL and Lowe was traded to another team. This turnover in defensive players left the Lions with a completely new secondary.

Immediately after his release from the club, it became apparent that none of the other NFL teams were interested in Richard as a player either. "I contacted them all by letter or phone call, but nothing ever came from it. I thought it was very unusual for someone with my background not to get another shot, but the chances were slim going in and I knew it."

Before Richard had too much time to fret about his being released from the team, he got another, more positive call. This one came from the Lions' owner, William Clay Ford. "Mr. Ford and I had always got along fine. I think he understood what it took for someone to make it in that league. And, I think he understood what obstacles a black man had to overcome."

Richard went to Ford's office and they had a brief discussion. Then Ford told Richard, "Dick, I need you to be in the front office. As my special assistant."

"What would my duties be?" Richard asked.

"You would help me with players' contracts, any disputes with the team, and do some scouting for us."

"Who would my boss be?"

"Just me. You answer to me," Ford responded.

"What about me coaching somewhere down the line?"

"You know I can't promise anything right now. The head coach still retains the ability to pick his coaches."

"I understand. When do you want my decision?"

"As soon as possible."

Both men shook hands and Richard left his office. It wasn't much later in the day before Richard knew he had to give it a chance. Not too many players went directly from the field to the front office, especially black players. He would be making big news in the league with this move.

The two met soon afterward and Richard took the post. It was a position he would hold for the next seven years. Although important, the position wouldn't fulfill Richard's dreams of being a head coach or even an assistant coach in the NFL.

Richard took the special staff assistant job and hit the ground running. "I did everything Mr. Ford wanted. I handled player contracts, player disputes, and any liaison Mr. Ford needed between his office and the team. Whenever there was a problem that the head coach couldn't handle, they just called me. I did all the dirty work."

But as the years passed, Richard found out the politics of the position made it unbearable. "I couldn't make everyone happy," he recalled. "I'd solve one problem today and the next day another variation of the same problem would jump up."

On top of all the day-to-day problems and politics, Richard came face to face with the underlying forces of racial bigotry. "It had always been there, but lots of guys didn't really say anything about it. Being black worked in many cases, but being a black in a big position of power just didn't do too well. Every white guy in the organization felt I had too much power and they felt threatened by my place in the system. I could finally see that racial bigotry would really limit me from learning and moving up the ladder."

Deep down inside, Richard really wanted to coach, but the cards were stacked against him. "Some guys said I didn't communicate too well when I played. All I can say is, look at our record. We did pretty well. Not great, but pretty good some years. I don't think I was to blame for all the bad times."

As time went by, Richard finally knew his chances of moving toward the coaching goal were minimal at best. "Sometimes I'd just go down on the field, you know, during games. The coaches didn't want me near the bench. I guess they thought I'd say something to take their power away."

It got to be just like his playing days, when he held out some years for a better salary. "I used to play some hardball with the management and hold out. I'd see that some guys younger than me, with less experience, white guys, would walk in and get better contracts. I used to think that holding out would pay off. Well, it didn't. I guess I finally realized that the front office job with Mr. Ford was another form of holding out. I was waiting for that coaching slot. It would never come."

Richard made several inquiries around the country into a college head coaching post, but his lack of a college degree put up an invisible stone wall. "Looking back at it, I know it was a huge mistake not getting my degree when I was young, but everyone makes mistakes."

One day, the dean at Southern University in Baton Rouge, Louisiana, called Richard and made him an offer. It was a pretty good one. The dean wanted him to coach the defense and report only to the head coach, Charley Bates. Richard worked out a deal with the dean. He'd take the job, if the school would let him return to school and finish his college education. "I knew this was a great opportunity and I wasn't going to pass it up."

After some discussion about benefits and so forth, the deal was made with Southern University. Richard then went to see Mr. Ford, to tell him he was leaving Detroit. "I was happy, but also sad. Mr. Ford had been fair with me in every respect and I knew I was doing him a good service, but I just wasn't happy about the limited chance to coach. We parted on good terms."

Southern University was a Division I AA school with lots of promise when Richard arrived for the 1972 year. "I showed up and was mentally prepared to hit it a full 100% for the team and school. I wanted to win and I wanted that degree."

But politics reared its ugly head again. Richard immediately had personality problems with head coach Charles Bates. "I really think Bates was intimidated by me," Richard said. "Here I was a big time NFL player and all. I just wanted to tell the kids about my experiences, my times on winning teams. Bates and I didn't hit it off too good. I'm not sure he even approved my coming to the school. The dean probably forced him into it."

Richard was paid $15,000 a year to be defensive coordinator, but it would have taken a lot more money to keep him at the school. "It was just terrible. I loved the kids, but Bates was always trying to make me look bad by not taking my advice." Richard wanted to instill a distinct structure within the team, a structure founded on confidence. "I wanted them to practice what I taught them. I didn't want any guess work on the field. Bates had other ideas. The end result was a disastrous record of 2-7-1."

At the end of the season, Richard resigned his position as defensive coordinator at Southern. But he made another college contact, this time in Wilberforce, Ohio, at Central State University. "Deep in my mind, I knew the NFL needed black coaches and I was just out to prove them wrong about not hiring me, but it backfired. I really didn't want a head coach's job in college. I wanted to bypass that route and go straight to the pros. My timing again was bad in Ohio, and I only lasted one season."

Chapter Twelve

ON THE ROAD WITH REDD

After Richard left his coaching position at Central State University in Wilberforce, Ohio, an old acquaintance of his—Redd Foxx—offered him a job. He had met the comedian through his deceased wife, Dinah Washington. Previously, in 1952, as Richard's reputation grew nationally in the NFL, he had the opportunity to meet Redd, who was making it big on the live concert level in local clubs across the country. It was not uncommon for sports stars to be "courted" by celebrities in the entertainment industry. Athletes enjoyed being around these famous people and the attention it attracted.

Once, while attending a comedy show in Los Angeles, Redd asked for Richard to come backstage so they could talk. Even through Redd's vulgar exterior it was easy to see he really cared about people. He and Richard immediately hit it off. "You have to remember," Richard said, "even though I really didn't consider myself anything special back then, I was making headlines across the sports pages and my name was a constant reminder of the black man's struggle to make it in a predominantly white society. Redd knew this and he made it a point to keep in touch with any black people in this arena."

Dinah Washington had died in 1963, and her untimely demise had stunned the black entertainment world. "Redd came up to me shortly after her death and said 'If the time comes, give me a call, I'll find something for you to do.' I really didn't put too much weight to it at that time, but several years later Redd heard about my retirement and he called me first."

Richard traveled to Los Angeles to meet with Redd at his home. "I knew he would probably offer me a job, but I didn't know exactly what it would be until we met face to face." During the informal meeting, Redd didn't pull any punches with Richard.

"Dick, listen to me. Dinah gave me a job when I couldn't get one and I'm gonna do the same for you. I want you to be my road manager," Redd said.

"What about the other people already with you?" Richard asked.

"They're mostly good people and all, but I want you around to handle my personal stuff. My bookings, my money, my payroll to my employees. And, I want you to act as my bodyguard too," Redd continued.

Richard sat there, not knowing what to say. Finally, he answered him. "Redd, I'll take the job. I don't have anything lined up now and it's perfect timing for me. When do you want me to start?"

Redd looked at him with a quizzical face before answering. "Hell, right now!" he exclaimed.

"Redd, I didn't bring any of my stuff from Detroit with me."

"Well, hell then, just go get it. I need you right now."

After that initial meeting, Richard flew back to Detroit to get his belongings and moved to Los Angeles. He went on to explain, "What happened long before I came into the picture was that Dinah's status as a famous celebrity enabled her to call lots of her own shots when it came to hiring and firing people at the black clubs. I knew for a fact that she demanded that certain performers get to work her shows just to enable them to get their name in the public eye. Dinah knew these performers couldn't command anything by themselves, but with her pull, she was able to get their names included as her opening acts."

Richard used to ask her why she did so much for these new performers.

"Honey, I'll continue to help them out when I can. Show business is tough and they don't care about anything except the almighty dollar," Dinah explained.

"But you're putting people on board that don't have much of a name," Richard countered.

"Yeah, but after I get through with them they will have a name. Lots of them have some good talent. They just haven't been discovered yet."

In the 1940s, 1950s, and 1960s the black industry was a tightly knit group of people who played to a much smaller audience than the overall white population. Even so, these entertainers commanded large sums of money and they performed weekly to huge audiences. Dinah Washington was no exception to this rule. She was one of the most famous black female singers of her time. When she did people favors, as she usually did, they normally didn't forget it, and when the time came they tried to help her or the people around her.

Once back in L.A. the real work started for Richard. Redd was moving up the entertainment ladder fast. His live shows were sold out and his comedy albums were selling at a brisk pace. "He was in demand every day of the week. The phone calls never seemed to stop. They all would pay almost anything to get him to perform in their clubs. Redd got to call all his own shots."

Richard jumped right into the middle of a whirlwind with the Redd Foxx tour. He handled all the money and payroll and any personal things Redd wanted handled that required a certain touch. "Redd had lots of girls around him," Richard recalled. "He just seemed to attract them everywhere he went. It was up to me to let certain ones get close to him before and after shows and to make sure the other ones didn't get near him." Once, when he was learning the ropes, a young woman came backstage and said Redd asked for her. When Richard escorted her to Redd's dressing room, he got a long stare from Redd.

"Train! What the hell you doin', man?" Redd yelled. "Get her out of here. She's crazy!"

"But Redd, I thought you wanted to see her," Richard said.

"No damn way!"

Richard turned around to look at the girl, who was slowly walking toward Redd. As Redd backed up, Richard grabbed her and pulled her out of the room. She yelled and screamed all the way. Once outside the room, Richard pushed her away and told her not to come back. When he walked back inside, Redd was waiting for him, ready to cuss him out.

"Redd, I'm really sorry, man."

"Oh hell, man. You didn't know. That girl has followed me a bunch of times. She's always trying to get backstage."

"How do I know when to let one in to see you?" Richard asked.

"You just ask me first. That's how."

"Okay, Redd, I got it."

After Richard had failed his first test as a Redd Foxx bodyguard, he made sure his future introductions were handled properly. But an even tougher obstacle lay ahead for him: handling all the money Redd generated. "Redd made lots of money back then and he had lots of 'leeches' trying to get a hold of him all of the time. I called them leeches because I couldn't see any other purpose they had but to suck the money from him."

Redd didn't help matters much in this regard either. He was known around town as a guy who would give you his last dime. "I recall some guys walking up to Redd while we were on the road and pulling out a wad of bills and giving them to him. They would say something like 'Thanks, Redd, I owed you this from two years ago.' It was real crazy, the way he handled his money."

Once, the Apollo Theater in New York City booked Redd for a solid week. He sold out every show every day of the week. Both the Apollo and Redd made a lot of money that week and they begged him to stay a few extra days, but he was already booked up in another city. "The Apollo was a great place to play. It was an old establishment with lots of history to it and many of the big time performers booked shows there over the years," Richard said. "It was a famous place, just like Yankee Stadium. Playing there was a feather in anyone's cap."

Redd required Richard to keep a daily log of everyone's expenses and activities. When he wanted to see what a particular person paid for something, he expected Richard to have it written down. "He was a sharp guy in that respect," Richard noted.

"He may have given money away on occasion, but when it came to running his end of the business, he wanted to be on top of it all."

Everyone always wondered if Redd was as funny in private as he was on stage. All the people around him never saw any difference between his stage act and his personal treatment of the people in his daily life. "He seemed to always call people 'dummy,' just like he called Demond Wilson on 'Sanford and Son.' Any time of the day or night, Redd could be funny in an instant. Whatever the situation, he had some funny remark about it. He never seemed be at a loss for humorous words."

The Redd Foxx entourage traveled by any means necessary to get to an engagement. "Sometimes the person booking Redd would arrange for a tour bus to pick us up and drive us to our destination, even if it was a long way off in another city. Other times, we'd fly at Redd's expense on a commercial flight, and on other occasions we'd all just jump into four large cars and drive to a certain city. There was never any rhyme or reason to it, just whatever the situation would bear."

Richard always called Redd "Zorro," due to his tendency to carry a large switchblade knife with him at all times. The knife made him feel safe and it gave him a kind of swagger to his demeanor. "I'm not sure when the knife first appeared, probably before I came into the picture," Richard noted. "But he never went anywhere without it. I once asked him why he didn't carry a bigger knife, since apparently he was scared of something."

"Train," Redd said, "you don't know a damn thing about show business, do you?"

"Apparently not, Redd."

"Just you take care of the things I want you to do and we'll be okay."

After that rebuttal from Redd, Richard never brought it up again, and Redd continued to carry the switchblade. "It was kind of like his personal trademark."

A lot of people didn't know it, but Redd arranged for some 10-year-old kids to travel with his tour group. These kids would open the shows and perform a tap dance routine that always amazed the audience. "Man, could those kids dance," Richard noted. "No matter how many times I saw them, they still could almost hypnotize you with their tap dancing abliity. I always wondered what happened to them later on in life."

The tap dancing kids attracted hundreds of kids who wanted to be like them. "Man, it was a big deal. A 10-year-old traveling with Redd Foxx. All the kids wanted to go with us," Richard said. "But Redd had to be careful about it. He was a big drinker and a smoker and it was my job to keep them away from all that. Redd never wanted to be criticized for having his kids around all that stuff. I constantly would catch them trying to sneak a smoke behind stage. I for sure didn't want any of their parents finding out about it."

Redd had also hired a young man who was about 23 years old. He was the son of a close friend of Redd's, and Redd wanted to do the guy a favor by hiring his son, even if he had no business traveling with the entourage. Richard called this kid "Big Stupid." He remembered, "This kid was just dumb. He and I just never hit it off from the outset. Big Stupid was always trying to pull something on me or Redd. I always caught him in some prank or shady operation. And it usually cost Redd money." Richard continued, "Well, Big Stupid was usually trying to do just the opposite of what Redd wanted him to do and I'd catch him doing wrong. I'd say, hey man, what you doing that for? Redd doesn't want any of that around here."

"Redd don't care," Big Stupid responded.

"The hell he don't," Richard countered back. "I know better than that and it's my job to keep this stuff straight."

"Why don't you just leave me alone, Train?"

" 'Cause Redd hired me to keep things going smooth and I ain't gonna put up with this stuff you been doing," Richard said. "Just keep doing it and I'll get your butt fired!"

"Oh, the hell with you, man. I was here before you and I'll be here later on too."

"Maybe so, but while I'm running the show, this ain't gonna work like this."

Richard noted, "It was always some con game with him. Redd would ask for something and Big Stupid would try to take the money and get it cheaper somewhere else. He thought he could get away with anything."

As the show traveled across the country for weeks at a time,

Redd made it a point to do shows for inmates at certain prisons. He had a relative who had done some hard time in prison, and he always had a soft spot in his heart for the inmates. "I always thought that was real nice of him, to entertain the cons that way," Richard said.

The show went to Rikkers Island Prison in New York, courtesy of an invitation from the governor of New York. Richard didn't like going into a prison to do a show, but Redd insisted on it. "Redd," Richard said, "why the hell we gotta go into a prison?"

"Me and the governor are pals and he asked me, that's why."

"Why did the governor pick Rikkers Island?"

"That's his deal," Redd responded. "I'm just along to make him happy. You can't ever tell when you'll need a favor from the governor of New York."

Richard noted, "You gotta remember, we all carried pistols, just like Redd carried his switchblade. Everybody was packing some heat back then. It was just standard for us." When the group arrived at Rikkers Island, they all piled out of their touring bus and Richard gave them a speech on leaving their pistols in the bus. "I told them, we can't be taking any guns into a prison. We'll just lock them up in the bus."

It seemed like everyone agreed, everyone but Big Stupid. As they all filed into the prison door, Big Stupid's gun set off the alarm. Guards came running from every direction. Redd was very upset about it all. In fact, he was more upset with Richard for letting it happen. "Train, what the hell you doing, man? I thought we all agreed to leave them in the bus. It's your job to make sure this doesn't happen!"

"Redd, what do you want me to do, search our own people?" Richard asked. "Big Stupid here knew what was happening. He's always doing something dumb."

"Train, you're in charge of our security. You got to watch out for stuff like this. It makes me look bad with the governor," Redd yelled back.

Toward the end of the argument, Richard turned to look at Big Stupid, who was standing all alone and not saying anything to anyone. "Man! Are you dumb or what? If those inmates ever got that gun, they'd use it on us and then they'd make you eat it! Go back outside and put the damn thing in the bus."

Later on, after the show inside the prison was progressing, Redd was keeping them all in stitches with his smart remarks. Everyone was laughing, even the warden and the guards. At one point during the show an inmate jumped up and yelled at Redd, "Hey, man! Do you remember me?"

Redd looked at him for a second and then replied, "Hell yeah, man! How you doing?"

"I need for you to give me a piece of the action!"

Redd stood there for a long pause, not really saying anything as the whole room had gone quiet. Finally, he waved at the guy and said, "Yeah, I'll give it to the warden!"

After the show Richard approached Redd about the inmate who yelled at him. "Who the hell was that? That dude who yelled at you?"

"I knew the guy. I didn't know he was in here," Redd replied.

"What you gonna do?"

"I'll do what I said I'd do. Give him a piece of the action."

Although Richard never saw him actually give the warden any money, Redd did walk off with the warden later and when he returned, Richard asked him about it. "You leave the guy some cash?"

"Just a little," Redd said, matter of factly.

Richard left it at that. He never found out how much money he left or who the guy was, since Redd didn't want to discuss it with him. Richard always felt it was some friend of Redd's who had fallen on some hard times and Redd was embarrassed by it.

On another visit to the Apollo Theater in New York, the show was going great and the crowd was really into it. While Richard and the rest of the entourage stood behind the curtains, Redd walked offstage and started taking off his clothes. Some of his entourage started laughing, while some of them just stood and looked at him. Richard walked up to him and said, "Redd, what the hell you doing, man?"

"I'm getting ready to streak!"

"What's the deal?"

"Remember when that guy streaked on me in L.A.?"

"Yeah," Richard replied.

"Well, it was funny as hell and I'm gonna do it too."

Richard and the rest of the crew stood there, slightly

shocked as Redd walked past the curtain, then started running across the stage. The crowd went wild as he ran and waved at them. Richard sarcastically remarked, "I guess you could call that a highlight of my career with Redd."

As the Redd Foxx tour grew in popularity, so did his ability to command top dollar. It was very common for Redd and his crew to play a particular hotel, club, or casino for a week, doing two or three shows per day and being paid from $50,000 to $70,000 for the entire week.

Richard recalled, "We played one of the largest hotels in Miami once, back in 1966. The manager literally begged Redd to show up and do his routine, but Redd told him on the phone that he was all booked up and the time he had scheduled off during that particular week he wanted to rest.

"Well, this manager tells Redd he will double his normal salary if he'll just do a three day gig. Plus, he said he'd pay for our airfare from Los Angeles to Miami. When Redd heard it was a week's salary for three days work, that convinced him."

When Redd toured the country, all of the club operators begged him to watch certain performers. They always assured him these performers would be qualified hits on the comedy circuit if he would just give them a break. Many times Redd would oblige them, knowing that the odds were heavily against these people ever making it in the industry. "Redd came up the hard way and he wanted to give any of the black people a break if he could. And, if the act was bad, Redd never said a word. He was a good guy in that respect."

After about a year on the road, Richard decided it was time to move on to another more promising career. He was offered a job with the Detroit Police Athletic League (PAL), and the timing was right for him to leave Redd Foxx. "I just felt Redd was a little unstable and he might decide to quit the business. And there was always the possibility that the business wouldn't want him anymore. It was just a situation that I felt uncomfortable with at that time of my life."

Chapter Thirteen

BACK IN THE
MOTOR CITY

Richard had a way with kids, especially underprivileged kids. He grew up in that type of environment and he was quick to adapt to their needs. The Detroit Athletic League, also known as the Police Athletic League (PAL), which was directly under the mayor's office, asked Richard to work with them. The Detroit mayor, Coleman Young, personally asked him to take the job.

Due to his work in Chicago with the youth programs, Richard had valuable experience in dealing with youth groups, speaking before large audiences, setting up athletic agendas and raising funds. After starting at the ground level of the Police Athletic League, he quickly moved up to the position of executive director, a very prestigious position. The PAL had replaced the Police and Youth in Sports program at the city level.

Richard recalled his position at the PAL in a very positive way. "Coleman Young, the city's mayor, had offered me this job and I wanted to do him right. So I put a 100% effort into it. Our program reached between 15,000 and 20,000 kids in the Detroit area. I was always very proud of that achievement. We had both civilians and some police officers working with us and some-times more than 1,000 volunteers."

Detroit had a huge inner city youth problem that was

caused by several factors, including lack of leadership for the various organizations, lack of funding to improve and expand the groups, and a lack of focus in expanding these facilities. Apparently, Coleman Young had the correct foresight to hire Richard, who would guide them through this maze.

In the early 1970s PAL offered 15 different athletic programs for boys and girls from the ages of 5 to 17, as well as individual tutoring and educational programs. "Our programs had various professional athletes in and around Detroit come in to work with us and to act as our spokespersons. We had professional people from the business world, such as Ford Motor Company representatives, General Motors representatives, Michigan Telephone Company people, and the Detroit School District administrators, work on our Board of Directors."

When Richard took over his position at PAL the organization was only five years old, growing at a steady pace, and in need of proper leadership. Over the next decade, Richard would be instrumental in achieving this goal.

Someone once asked Richard why he put so much effort into the PAL job. He quickly set them straight by saying, "I was thrown away as a kid and I never forgot it. That's a terrible feeling for a kid to have to live with. If I can make them feel better about themselves, well, I've done them a good deed."

Richard wielded a free hand at PAL and the system prospered for it. He was in charge of raising funds, overall development of programs, and overseeing the sports activities. But problems persisted in PAL just as they did everywhere else in the real world. "I think if I had more outside support from various groups, I could have made a bigger contribution to the community," he said. "You've always got to remember, young kids are restless and it's always a struggle to keep them on the straight and narrow. PAL was a preventative operation. We tried to keep them out of trouble. Money was usually the key."

Commenting on the past business of pro athletes giving back to the community, Richard noted, "It for sure is tougher for us. The pro athletes used to come out and speak to all the kids, but today they seem to just give them some free tickets. I think the pros should always explain to them how they made it to the top. That's very important for a kid to understand."

Richard noted that he didn't get to see enough of the kids on a personal level. "The best way to interact with kids is being with them daily. That way you can gauge their feelings and whether you're reaching them or not. By me sitting behind a desk, it really stopped me from achieving this goal, but overall I guess it worked."

Richard was considered by most to be the innovator behind the football and hockey programs. "Of course, football was my pet at PAL, but I took just as much pride in the hockey and basketball programs. We even took credit for a #1 NBA draft pick—Derrick Coleman. He started with us in Detroit. Derrick was a great kid."

PAL and its predecessor programs were set up to take the place of shortcomings in the city's education programs. "It was apparent the normal educational duties in the schools were not achieving their overall goals. Especially the summer periods when school was not able to reach them. We tried to do it." He also noted, "It's hard to talk about it, but many of the kids' parents also were at fault. For various reasons they didn't instruct their children properly and problems ensued."

In all inner-city settings, the drug and crime problems were paramount. Detroit was no exception. "I can't overemphasize the impact drugs had on some kids. They got caught up in it and couldn't get out. It was a never-ending cycle."

The leadership at PAL seemed to always be in a struggle to keep people and certain organizations from having unneeded conflicts. "We had enough problems to overcome. We for sure didn't need unnecessary confrontations between people at various levels of authority. Those types of problems just filtered down to the kids."

Richard pointed out that lack of education didn't have to be a minus in life. "There are many kids everywhere that will never make it to college. Some don't apply themselves properly, some have to work to help their families, and some aren't motivated toward a higher education. Our group took the place of those shortcomings in many instances."

Chapter Fourteen

FINAL COMMENTS

Any final comments on his past accomplishments and the future of the game of football should be reserved for the man himself, Richard "Night Train" Lane. "I've heard all those stories about me being a dirty player for years, and to tell you the truth, I've resented them," he said. "I was a hard-nosed player, that played within the rules, not a dirty player that played outside the rules of the game.

"You've always got to remember, to make it in the NFL, not only did you have to have the skills and determination, you had to be tough to survive. It was a dog-eat-dog world. I never tried to purposely hurt anyone. But if someone was going to get hurt, I didn't want it to be me."

About today's game and players in the new era, Richard noted, "I don't think most of them realize how guys in my time sacrificed to make the game what it is. Back then it was very difficult to make even $20,000 a year. And, in the off-season guys had to work hard, physical jobs to make ends meet. We didn't train year round either, partly due to our jobs and the fact that the team management didn't really push us that way."

Richard continued his explanation. "The money that's

being made today is gigantic, and believe me, if I had the chance I'd take it too. In today's terms, with my playing ability, I'd need two agents to handle all my negotiations. But I'm not trying to blow my own horn. I'm just saying something that would be fairly obvious. My highest salary was with the Lions and it totaled $25,000. Can you imagine? Living on $25,000? But, there were many, many guys with me all those years. Guys who played their hearts out and who had terrible injuries and they didn't get paid either. I was just one of several hundred who laid the foundation for today's game."

Richard made a comment about today's drug and alcohol use. "Drugs really weren't a problem in my time. Alcohol was always a problem in the sports world as it is in society and it will continue to be a problem. Alcohol ruins many lives every year. The players today can afford drugs, so it's just another temptation for them. I think any problem like that is just lack of commitment, integrity, or a personality weakness."

It was noted by many observers that when Richard was inducted into the Hall of Fame, some of his remarks were bitter and his comments hurt many people's feelings. "During my induction I said some things that maybe I shouldn't have said, but I'm a black American that came up in a tough society in a very tough and competitive job selection—playing pro football. Most of my comments were directed toward the people in power. The people who spend the money. The people who have held back the progress of the black Americans."

He was also very adamant about making one important point. "The pension we get today is a total farce. It's outrageous. I don't think it's asking too much for retired players like myself to get $2,000 a month to live on, instead of the few hundred bucks we get. The NFL commissioner should be ashamed that with today's money and TV contracts, he won't help the guys who started this league."

Richard commented about the future of pro football by saying, "The game itself will endure and probably develop in a positive manner. The game never really changes much, just a few rule changes and the fact that the faces behind the masks change every year." He also made a statement about the TV contracts and the open disclosure rules. "It looks like the players have finally been able to open up the owners' financial books for public observation. That's a good thing for them. Back in the early days, the owners would have hid every dollar they could so they could hold it back from us. But the TV contracts opened it up, along with the huge dollars being generated. I hope the guys playing today make as much as they can. Because you never know when it will be over."

BIBLIOGRAPHY

BOOKS:

National Football League Properties. *The Official 1996 NFL Record and Fact Book.* NFL Properties Inc., Publishing Group, Los Angeles, Calif., 1996.

NEWSPAPERS AND MAGAZINES:

American Statesman (1994)
Black Sports Magazine (1974)
Sports Collectors Digest (1995)
Detroit Free Press (1965, 1973)
Detroit News (1962, 1972)
Los Angeles Herald Examiner (1962, 1963)
Chicago American (1963)
Washington Post (1962)
Chicago Tribune (1983)

OTHER SOURCES:

National Football League. Hall of Fame Archives, Canton, Ohio.
Detroit Police Athletic League (PAL). Detroit, Michigan.

www.ingramcontent.com/pod-product-compliance
Lightning Source LLC
Chambersburg PA
CBHW051729090426
42738CB00010B/2158

* 9 7 8 1 5 7 1 6 8 4 4 0 0 *